Gooseberry Patch co.®

A Country Store In Your Mailbox®

Blue Plate Specials

A Country Store In Your Mailbox®

Gooseberry Patch
600 London Road
Department Book
Delaware, OH 43015
★
1-800-854-6673
gooseberrypatch.com

Copyright 2001, Gooseberry Patch 1-888052-94-5
First Printing, November, 2001

How To Subscribe

Would you like to receive
"A Country Store in Your Mailbox"®?
For a 2-year subscription to our 96-page
Gooseberry Patch catalog, simply send $3.00 to:

Gooseberry Patch
600 London Road
Delaware, OH 43015

Contents

Dedication

To everyone who enjoys a juicy
burger with a side of shoestring
fries at the local diner.

Appreciation

Thanks to all of our Gooseberry
Patch friends & family who
shared their favorite recipes
for this very special book.

Eat Here!

LOBSTER LOUIE'S

A taste of New England's finest.

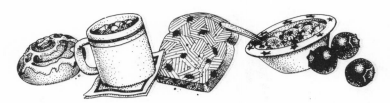

Frosted Cinnamon Rolls

Emily Buchanan
Grand Junction, CO

*Try sprinkling with raisins or chopped pecans
just before rolling and slicing.*

1-2/3 c. sugar, divided
3 c. warm water
2 t. salt
2/3 c. shortening
3 pkgs. active dry yeast

3 eggs
8 to 9 c. all-purpose flour
1-1/2 t. cinnamon
3 T. butter, melted

Blend 2/3 cup sugar, water, salt and shortening together in a large mixing bowl; add yeast. Mix in eggs; gradually add flour. Knead thoroughly; place dough in large greased bowl. Cover and let rise until double in bulk. In a small mixing bowl, combine remaining sugar, cinnamon and butter; roll dough into a 15"x10" rectangle. Spread cinnamon mixture over the top; roll up jelly roll-style and cut into one-inch slices. Place on a greased baking sheet; let rise. Bake at 350 degrees until light brown; cool until warm to the touch. Generously coat tops with frosting. Makes about 2 dozen.

Frosting:

1/4 c. butter, softened
3 c. powdered sugar
1 t. vanilla extract

3 T. whipping cream
Optional: maple flavoring to
taste

Blend together butter and powdered sugar; stir in vanilla, cream and maple flavoring, if desired. Blend with an electric mixer on medium speed until light and fluffy.

On the next family vacation, give everyone a disposable
camera and a manila folder for ticket stubs, brochures and
postcards...use these souvenirs to create a memory book.

LOBSTER
LOUIE'S

New England Blueberry Coffee Cake

Linda Hensz
Beach Lake, PA

*This coffee cake is so delicious...I never have leftovers when
I take it to church or get-togethers.*

1-1/2 c. all-purpose flour
1/2 c. sugar
1 T. baking powder
1 t. cinnamon
1/2 t. salt

1-1/2 c. blueberries
1 egg
1/2 c. milk
1/4 c. butter, melted

Combine dry ingredients together; gently fold in blueberries and set
aside. Whisk egg, milk and butter together in a small mixing bowl; add
to flour mixture, stirring carefully. Pour into a greased 8"x8" baking
pan; sprinkle with topping. Bake at 425 degrees for 20 to 25 minutes.
Makes 12 servings.

Topping:

1/4 c. butter, melted
3/4 c. brown sugar, packed

1 T. all-purpose flour
Optional: 1/2 c. chopped walnuts

Combine ingredients; mix well.

The diner is everybody's kitchen.
– Richard Gutman

Fireside Coffee

June Gravitte
Renfrew, PA

Fill Mason jars full and give as gifts.

2 c. hot chocolate mix
2 c. non-dairy creamer
1 c. instant coffee granules

1-1/2 c. sugar
1 t. cinnamon
1 t. nutmeg

Shake ingredients together; store in an airtight container. Stir desired amount into a mug of hot water or milk. Makes 6-1/2 cups mix.

Minty Hot Cocoa

Cheri Monsen
Monument, CO

So creamy and chocolatey!

1 c. powdered milk
1 c. sugar
1/4 c. hot chocolate mix

1/4 c. mint chocolate chips
1/2 c. mini marshmallows

Mix together all ingredients; store in an airtight container. Use 2/3 cup boiling water to 1/3 cup mix. Makes 8 servings.

Yummy coffee and cocoa mixes are not only fun to give but they're great to take along on family camping trips! Pack a thermos of hot water for an on-the-road treat.

LOBSTER LOUIE'S

Oven-Baked French Toast

Lynda McCormick
Burkburnett, TX

*Before baking, set this moist French toast in the
refrigerator overnight to absorb all the flavors.*

16-oz. loaf French bread
2 c. cranberries, divided
2 T. sugar
1 t. vanilla extract

1/4 t. cinnamon
8 eggs
1/2 c. milk
1-1/2 c. maple syrup

Slice bread into eight, 3/4-inch thick slices; lay on a lightly greased
13"x9" baking sheet. Scatter one cup cranberries over the slices; blend
sugar, vanilla, cinnamon, eggs and milk together. Pour over bread; let
stand 15 minutes. Lift bread slices a bit so egg mixture will moisten
undersides; cover and refrigerate overnight. Uncover; bake at
350 degrees for 40 minutes. While bread bakes, bring maple syrup
and remaining cranberries to a boil; reduce heat to low and cook
10 minutes. Serve warm over bread. Makes 8 servings.

**For whimsical giftwrap, wrap up a special package with a
vintage road map or use a colorful map from a theme park!**

Burst-of-Lemon Muffins

Polly Sonowski
Wooster, OH

These sweet muffins are perfect for tucking in lunch boxes.

1-3/4 c. all-purpose flour
3/4 c. sugar
1 t. baking powder
3/4 t. baking soda
1/4 t. salt
8-oz. carton lemon yogurt

1 egg
1/3 c. butter, melted
1 T. lemon juice
2 T. lemon zest
1/2 c. flaked coconut
Optional: 1/2 c. poppy seed

Combine first 5 ingredients; set aside. In a large mixing bowl, mix remaining ingredients together; stir in dry ingredients. Spoon into muffin tins lined with baking cups; bake at 400 degrees for 18 to 22 minutes. Let muffins cool for 5 minutes; remove from pans. Pierce muffin tops; spoon topping over each muffin before serving. Makes one dozen.

Topping:

1/3 c. lemon juice
1/4 c. sugar

1/4 c. flaked coconut, toasted

Stir lemon juice and sugar in a saucepan over medium heat until sugar dissolves. Remove from heat; fold in coconut.

I think it is all a matter of love:
the more you love a memory, the stronger and stronger it is.
–Vladimir Nabokov

LOBSTER LOUIE'S

Cranberry Bread

Suzy Skaggs
San Angelo, TX

Don't wait for Thanksgiving to enjoy this delicious, tart-sweet bread!

1 c. sugar
2 T. margarine, melted
1 egg
3/4 c. orange juice
1 c. all-purpose flour
1 c. whole-wheat flour

1/2 t. salt
1/2 t. baking soda
1-1/2 t. baking powder
1 c. chopped pecans
1 c. cranberries
Garnish: powdered sugar

Blend all ingredients together except pecans, cranberries and powdered sugar; mix well. Fold in pecans and cranberries; pour into a greased 9"x5" loaf pan. Bake at 350 degrees for one hour; dust with powdered sugar. Makes 8 servings.

To unwind after a busy week, relax with your favorite old shows. Make a pail of popcorn on the stovetop...spend an afternoon watching classic TV shows like *I Love Lucy*, *The Honeymooners*, *The Mickey Mouse Club* and don't use the remote!

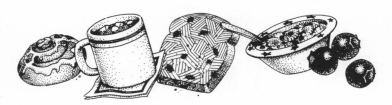

Maryland Cream Waffles

Carolyn Stewart
Crescent Springs, KY

Try topping these fluffy waffles with fresh berries or apple slices.

2 c. all-purpose flour
4 t. baking powder
1/2 t. salt
2 t. sugar

1-3/4 c. milk
2 eggs, separated and beaten
1/2 c. butter, melted

Mix dry ingredients together; add milk and egg yolks. Blend in melted butter; gently fold in stiffly beaten egg whites. Lightly grease a heated waffle iron; add batter and heat according to waffle iron's instructions. Makes 4 to 5 servings.

Cranberry Tea

Paulette Stewart
Omaha, NE

This is my mom's recipe...it's a tradition at our house!

1 cinnamon stick
1 t. whole cloves
1-1/2 c. sugar
2 qts. water

6 teabags
1 c. orange juice
juice of 2 lemons
3 drops red food coloring

Place spices and water in a saucepan; boil for 5 minutes. Remove from heat; add teabags and let steep one hour. Remove cinnamon stick and all but 6 cloves; add remaining ingredients and heat thoroughly. Discard remaining cloves before serving. Makes 6 to 8 servings.

Look for vintage towels and tablecloths with your state's regional characteristics like lobsters and lighthouses in New England.

LOBSTER LOUIE'S

Crisp Banana Waffles

Jan Hansen
Astoria, OR

*Sprinkle with chopped nuts and drizzle with warm
maple syrup...mmm!*

1 c. all-purpose flour	2 T. sugar
2 t. baking powder	2 eggs, separated
1/2 t. salt	1 c. milk
1/4 t. cinnamon	1 c. banana, mashed
1/4 t. nutmeg	6 T. butter, melted

Blend flour, baking powder, salt, cinnamon, nutmeg and sugar
together; set aside. Beat egg yolks and milk together; add flour
mixture, stirring until just blended. Fold in banana and melted butter;
mix well. In a small mixing bowl, beat egg whites until stiff and
peaks form; gently fold into batter. Bake on a waffle iron following
manufacturer's instructions. Serves 4.

Travel tip: Have fun playing Auto Watch. Everyone chooses a
different automobile by make, model or color...the person who
spots the most cars in his or her category in
20 minutes is the winner.

Baked Clam Dip

Jessica Ytuarte
Whittier, CA

Slice a second loaf of sourdough bread for dipping.

1 round loaf sourdough bread
2 6-1/2 oz. cans minced clams,
   drained
1/2 c. clam juice
2 8-oz. pkgs. cream cheese,
   softened

1 T. fresh parsley, chopped
1 t. lemon juice
10 drops hot pepper sauce
garlic salt to taste

Hollow out bread round; cube removed bread and set aside. Mix remaining ingredients together; spoon into bread round. Double wrap loaf in aluminum foil; place on a baking sheet. Bake at 350 degrees for 2 hours. Remove cover and serve warm with remaining cubed bread. Makes 4 cups.

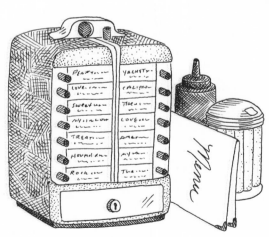

**Travel is ninety percent anticipation and
ten percent recollection.
– Edward Streeter**

LOBSTER LOUIE'S

Shrimp Ball

Theone Neel
Bastian, VA

"Shrimply" delightful...a taste of the sea in a cheesy appetizer!

2 6-oz. pkgs. frozen cooked
   small shrimp, thawed
2 8-oz. pkgs. cream cheese,
   softened
1 t. onion, minced

1/4 t. garlic salt
1/2 t. hot pepper sauce
2 T. mayonnaise
salt to taste
2 T. fresh parsley, chopped

Pat shrimp with paper towel to remove excess moisture; set aside.
Combine cream cheese, onion, garlic salt, hot pepper sauce,
mayonnaise and salt; mix well. Fold in shrimp; form into a ball and
wrap in plastic wrap. Chill; sprinkle with parsley before serving. Makes
about 3-1/2 cups.

**Don't pass up national parks on your next road trip. Many
offer daily activities for the whole family including guided
hikes and wildlife tours. Best of all, most are free!**

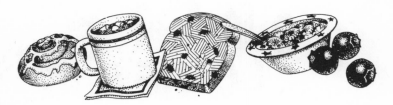

Crabbies

Joan Lachance
Saco, ME

*Serve these crunchy, crabby treats for lunch or cut
into quarters for appetizers.*

6-oz. can crabmeat, drained
5-oz. jar sharp pasteurized
   process cheese spread
1/2 c. butter, softened

1-1/2 t. mayonnaise
1/4 t. garlic powder
1/2 t. salt
6 English muffins, split in half

Mix all ingredients together except English muffins; spread on muffin halves. Cut muffin halves into quarters; broil until golden brown and bubbly, about 5 to 6 minutes. Makes 2 dozen.

Enjoy the fun of the diner at home! Include a napkin dispenser, sugar shaker, salt & pepper, creamer, red and yellow squirt bottles and, of course, a menu with today's special!

LOBSTER LOUIE'S

Crab-Swiss Bites

Cindi Manuel
York, PA

A touch of Swiss makes these snacks a cheesy treat.

6-oz. can crabmeat
1 T. onion, grated
1/2 c. shredded Swiss cheese
1/2 c. mayonnaise

1 t. lemon juice
12-oz. pkg. refrigerated flaky
  biscuits

Combine first five ingredients; set aside. Divide biscuits into three layers each; place on a greased baking sheet. Spoon crab mixture on top; bake at 400 degrees for 10 to 12 minutes. Makes 30.

Tangy Tartar Sauce

Mary Bettuchy
Duxbury, MA

You'll relish this creamy topping...so good on seafood!

1 c. mayonnaise
1/3 c. pickle relish
2 T. onion, minced

1 t. lemon juice
2 drops hot pepper sauce

Combine mayonnaise and relish; stir in remaining ingredients. Cover and refrigerate before serving. Makes about 1-1/2 cups.

For your next trip to a diner, learn some diner slang like mayo, stack (of pancakes) and BLT.

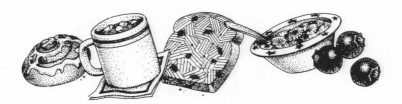

Corn & Pepper Relish

Kathleen Jones
Newburyport, MA

As a young girl, my mother and I would make different kinds of relish together...this is one of my favorites!

1 c. frozen corn, partially thawed
1 red pepper, chopped
1 green pepper, chopped
2 c. onion, chopped
1/2 c. sugar

1/2 t. turmeric
1/2 t. celery seed
1/2 t. mustard seed
1/4 t. salt
1 c. cider vinegar

Toss corn, peppers and onion together; set aside. Combine remaining ingredients in a one-quart saucepan; boil for 2 minutes. Immediately pour over vegetable mixture; cool. Refrigerate in airtight containers; use within 2 weeks. Makes four, 10-ounce jars.

Each day of our lives we make deposits
in the memory banks of our children.
– Charles R. Swindoll

LOBSTER LOUIE'S

Friday Night Sandwiches

Cathy Whittemore
Vassalboro, ME

*For the landlubbers in your family, substitute
cooked chicken for the crabmeat.*

6-oz. can crabmeat
2 stalks celery, finely chopped
2 green onions, finely chopped
4-oz. can sliced mushrooms,
    drained
1 t. caraway seed

1-1/2 T. mayonnaise
1-1/2 T. sour cream
4 slices bread, toasted
8 slices bacon, crisply cooked
4 slices Swiss cheese

Mix together first seven ingredients; spread over bread slices. Cover
with bacon and Swiss cheese; heat under broiler until cheese melts.
Makes 4 servings.

Fruit Smoothie

*Camille Simons
Richardson, TX*

A chilly treat that'll be welcome anytime!

2 c. milk
1/2 c. orange juice
8-oz. carton vanilla yogurt

1 banana, sliced
1 c. strawberries
1 c. crushed ice

Combine all ingredients in a blender until smooth. Makes 4 servings.

**Go off the beaten path on your next trip. You can find
farmers' markets, museums full of local history and
family-owned diners that you might otherwise have missed!**

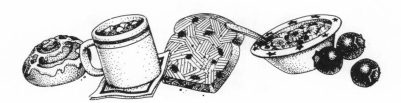

Classic Macaroni Salad

Rita Morgan
Pueblo, CO

This picnic favorite is a welcome addition to any get-together.

8-oz. pkg. elbow macaroni, cooked and drained
1/2 c. celery, chopped
1 onion, chopped
1 t. dried parsley
2 carrots, coarsely grated
6 hard-boiled eggs, peeled and chopped

1-1/2 c. sugar
1-1/2 c. water
1/4 c. all-purpose flour
1/2 c. vinegar
1/2 t. salt
1 c. mayonnaise
1/4 c. mustard

Combine macaroni, celery, onion, parsley, carrots and eggs; set aside. Boil next 5 ingredients until sugar and flour dissolve; allow to cool. Stir in mayonnaise and mustard; pour over macaroni mixture. Mix well; refrigerate before serving. Makes 10 to 15 servings.

Get together with neighbors and head to the local park for a dinner picnic. The kids play, the grown-ups talk and everyone eats great homemade food...just like the good ol' days.

LOBSTER LOUIE'S

Stuffed Chicken Salad Sandwiches

Martee Trepanier
Iron Mountain, MI

Try using leftover turkey in place of the shredded chicken...so yummy!

2 chicken breasts, cooked and
 shredded
1/2 c. mayonnaise-type salad
 dressing
1/4 c. onion, chopped

1/8 c. celery, chopped
1/8 c. water chestnuts, chopped
1/4 c. dried cranberries
1/4 c. chopped nuts
12 dinner rolls

Mix all ingredients together except dinner rolls; set aside. Slice and remove tops of rolls; scoop out centers. Fill rolls with chicken mixture; replace tops. Makes 12 servings.

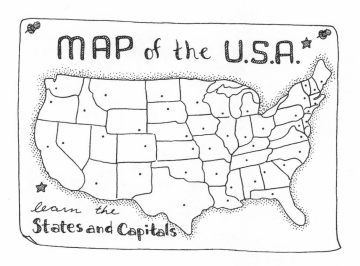

MAP of the U.S.A.

learn the **States and Capitals**

For some old-fashioned fun, rent a turnpike cruiser and go on a road trip or rent a roadster and cruise the town...put the top down!

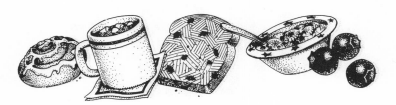

Cheddar Bites

The Governor's Inn
Ludlow, VT

Basically a French pastry which, with the addition of Vermont Cheddar cheese, becomes the perfect appetizer.

1 c. butter
2 c. milk
2 t. salt
2 c. all-purpose flour

8 eggs
1 c. Cheddar cheese, grated
2 T. fresh chives, chopped

Bring butter, milk and salt to a boil; remove from heat. Beat flour in with a wooden spoon; add eggs, one at a time, beating with an electric mixer after each addition. Stir in cheese and chives; drop tablespoonfuls of dough onto a greased baking sheet. Bake at 325 degrees for 35 minutes. Makes about 2 dozen.

I've run more risk eating my way across the country
than in all my driving.
– Duncan Hines

LOBSTER LOUIE'S

Creamy Potato-Clam Bisque

Corinne Gross
Tigard, OR

*Our family loves this chowder-type soup...when
I serve it to company, I'm always asked for the recipe.*

1/4 c. butter
1 onion, chopped
1 c. celery, chopped
4 slices bacon, crisply cooked
    and crumbled
1/8 c. fresh parsley, chopped
1/2 t. salt

1/4 t. pepper
4 potatoes, diced
1 qt. chicken broth
3 T. cornstarch
1/4 c. water
1 qt. half-and-half
3 6-oz. cans clams, undrained

Sauté butter, onion, celery and bacon for 10 minutes; add parsley, salt, pepper, potatoes and broth. Cover and cook for 30 minutes. Whisk cornstarch and water together; add half-and-half and clams. Pour into broth; simmer until heated thoroughly without boiling. Serves 6 to 8.

**Enjoy the simple fun of yesterday...invite friends over
for a game of bridge, poker or gin rummy.**

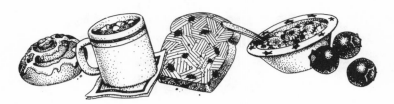

Blue Cheese Salad

Nicole Shira
New Baltimore, MI

The sweet, tangy blend of flavors in this salad is a great complement to grilled steak.

1 head lettuce, torn
11-oz. can mandarin oranges,
    drained
1 Granny Smith apple, peeled,
    cored and chopped

1/2 c. chopped walnuts
1/2 c. crumbled blue cheese
3 T. vinegar
1/2 c. oil
2 T. sugar

Toss first 4 ingredients together; set aside. Combine remaining ingredients; mix well. Pour over salad right before serving. Makes 6 to 8 servings.

Large potato chip tins are common flea market finds and many have charming retro graphics...use them to store your hot cocoa packets, teabags or cookie cutters.

LOBSTER LOUIE'S

Cape Cod Chowder

Caroline Capper
Circleville, OH

This soup is so quick & easy to fix and the ingredients are all things we usually have on hand. You can use any fish...we like cod best.

1 onion, chopped
4 T. butter
3 potatoes, diced
2 t. salt
1/2 t. dried basil
1/4 t. pepper

2 c. water
1 lb. frozen cod or haddock
    fillets, partly thawed
10-oz. pkg. frozen corn
12-oz. can evaporated milk

Sauté onion in butter until tender in a large Dutch oven; add potatoes, salt, basil, pepper and water. Simmer 15 minutes; place fillets on top and simmer 15 minutes more or until fish flakes easily. Stir in corn and evaporated milk; heat just to boiling. Ladle into heated bowls. Serves 4.

LUNCH *now* BEING SERVED

Remember when a great treat was a trip to the lunch counter at the old Woolworth's store downtown?

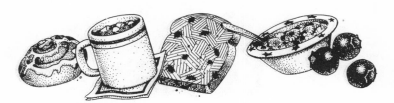

Cranberry Relish

Rita Rouse
Ballinger, TX

This relish is thick, creamy and tastes great!

2 c. cranberries
1 onion, chopped
3/4 c. sour cream

2 T. prepared horseradish
1/2 c. sugar

Grind cranberries and onion together in a food processor; add remaining ingredients and mix well. Freeze; thaw in refrigerator one hour before serving. Makes about 3-1/2 cups.

Serve your fluffy hotcakes or waffles with flair...instead of setting a plastic bottle on the table, serve warm syrup in small cream pitchers or a vintage syrup server.

LOBSTER LOUIE'S

Chicken Croquettes

Wendy Lee Paffenroth
Pine Island, NY

I found this dish in my great aunt's recipe box. I can still remember her making these for me when I was very young.

1/3 c. butter
1/2 c. all-purpose flour
1/2 t. salt
1/2 t. paprika
1-1/2 c. milk
2 egg yolks, beaten
1/2 c. whipping cream

1-1/2 c. cooked chicken, shredded
2 T. fresh parsley, chopped
1-1/2 c. bread crumbs
1 egg, beaten
2 T. water
oil for deep-frying

Melt butter in a double boiler; blend in flour and seasonings. Add milk; stir constantly until thickened. In a separate mixing bowl, blend egg yolks and cream; add to flour mixture and cook 3 minutes, stirring constantly. Add chicken and parsley; remove from heat and pour onto a platter. Cover with wax paper; chill for one to 2 hours. Shape chicken mixture into 3-inch rolls; coat in bread crumbs and set aside. Combine egg and water together; dip chicken into water mixture and then into remaining bread crumbs. Deep-fry in oil until golden brown; drain on paper towels. Serve hot with white sauce. Makes 1-1/2 dozen.

White Sauce:

2 T. butter
2 T. all-purpose flour
1/2 t. salt

1/8 t. pepper
1 c. milk

Melt butter in small skillet; blend in flour, salt and pepper. Gradually pour in milk. Stir until mixture boils and thickens.

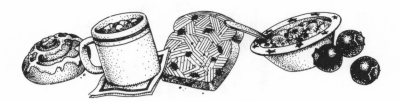

Zippy Clam Linguine

Vicki Hughes
Joliet, MT

For a richer, thicker sauce, stir in a little whipping cream.

2 green onions, chopped
3 cloves garlic, chopped
1/4 c. olive oil, divided
1/4 c. margarine
1 pt. cherry tomatoes, chopped
1/2 t. hot pepper sauce
1/2 t. Italian herb seasoning

2 6-1/2 oz. cans minced clams, drained
16-oz. pkg. linguine, cooked and drained
Garnish: freshly grated Parmesan cheese

Sauté onion and garlic in 2 tablespoons oil until tender; add remaining oil, margarine, tomatoes, hot pepper sauce and Italian seasoning. Reduce heat and simmer until tomatoes are cooked down; add clams. Heat thoroughly; pour over pasta. Sprinkle with Parmesan cheese. Makes 6 servings.

Remember the 1950's by sharing a malt with a friend...one glass, two straws!

LOBSTER
LOUIE'S

Angel Hair Pasta with Crabmeat

Sharon Walton
Lancaster, OH

Simply serve this dish with a salad and garlic bread,
and dinner's ready!

1 t. garlic, minced
1/3 c. green onions, chopped
6 T. margarine
6-oz. can crabmeat, rinsed and
    drained

1 c. whipping cream
12-oz. pkg. angel hair pasta,
    cooked and drained
1/2 c. fresh Parmesan cheese,
    grated

Sauté garlic and onion in margarine until tender; add crabmeat and whipping cream. Heat until thickened, stirring often. Pour over pasta; toss with Parmesan cheese before serving. Serves 4.

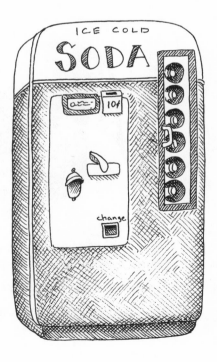

Change is inevitable, except
from a vending machine.
– Unknown

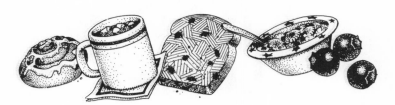

Pantry Pot Roast

Ethel Shires
Slidell, LA

This simple but delicious recipe is made with ingredients you probably have in the pantry.

2 to 3-lb. chuck roast
3/4 c. all-purpose flour
1 onion, sliced

10-1/2 oz. can beef broth
10-3/4 oz. can cream of mushroom soup

Coat roast with flour; brown in a large Dutch oven. Add onion slices; sauté until tender. Pour in broth, soup and 2 soup cans of water; bring to a boil. Reduce heat, cover and simmer 2 to 3 hours. Serves 4 to 6.

Keep a disposable camera in your glove box to capture the most memorable vacation moments. From sunsets to smiling faces, you won't miss a single one!

LOBSTER LOUIE'S

Refrigerator Rolls

Lisa Hays
Crocker, MO

Creamy mashed potatoes make these rolls moist and tender...they'll melt in your mouth!

1 pkg. active dry yeast
1-1/2 c. warm water
3/4 c. shortening
3/4 c. sugar

2 eggs
1 c. potatoes, mashed and warm
6-1/2 c. all-purpose flour
1 t. salt

Dissolve yeast in water; set aside. Cream shortening and sugar together; add eggs and blend until smooth. Mix in potatoes; blend in yeast mixture. In a separate bowl, sift flour and salt together; gradually add to yeast mixture. Cover; place in refrigerator until double in bulk. Punch down dough; divide into 36 portions. Roll into desired shapes; place on baking sheets. Let rise until double in bulk; bake at 350 degrees for 30 minutes or until golden brown. Makes 3 dozen.

Inexpensive aluminum pots & pans found at yard sales and flea markets are great for camping trips.

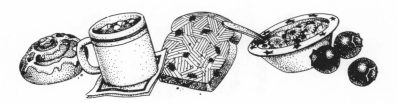

Patriotic Bread

Michelle Campen
Peoria, IL

*This scrumptious bread shows its true colors with tart,
red cranberry sauce and fresh, sweet blueberries.*

3 c. all-purpose flour
1 t. baking soda
1 t. baking powder
1 t. salt
1 c. sugar

1/2 c. butter, softened
2 eggs
1 c. buttermilk
1 c. whole-berry cranberry sauce
1 c. blueberries

Combine flour, baking soda, baking powder and salt; set aside. Cream sugar and butter together in a large mixing bowl; blend in eggs and buttermilk. Add flour mixture; mix well. Stir in cranberry sauce and blueberries; pour into a greased 9"x5" loaf pan. Bake at 375 degrees for one hour and 10 minutes or until a toothpick inserted in the center comes out clean. Remove from pan; cool on a wire rack. Makes 8 servings.

Blueberry Butter

Karen Moran
Navasota, TX

*Spread on your favorite breads and muffins
or even on unfrosted cake.*

3 pts. blueberries
4 c. apples, peeled, cored and
  coarsely chopped
4 c. sugar

1/2 t. cinnamon
1/8 t. mace
1/8 t. allspice
1/8 t. nutmeg

Combine ingredients in a heavy saucepan; heat over low heat until sugar dissolves, stirring often. Increase heat to medium-high; bring to a boil, stirring constantly. Reduce heat to low; continue simmering until mixture is thick, about 45 to 50 minutes, stirring often. Divide and pour into four, one-pint jars. Cover and keep refrigerated up to 2 weeks.

LOBSTER LOUIE'S

Creamy Gelatin

Jill Haddad
East Peoria, IL

Fruity gelatin is topped with a rich, creamy layer...a great dessert to serve to guests.

1 lb. cranberries
3 c. water
1-1/4 c. sugar, divided
20-oz. can crushed pineapple, drained, juice reserved
2 6-oz. pkgs. strawberry gelatin

3 c. boiling water
1 egg yolk
2 T. all-purpose flour
1 c. butter
1/2 c. chopped pecans

Grind cranberries with water in a blender; drain well. Add one cup sugar; let stand 2 hours. Stir in drained pineapple; mix and set aside. Dissolve gelatin in boiling water; cool. Stir into cranberry mixture; pour into serving dish. Refrigerate until completely set. Add enough water to reserved pineapple juice to equal one cup; mix together with remaining sugar, egg yolk, flour and butter. Pour into a saucepan; bring to a boil. Allow to cool; spread over gelatin and refrigerate. Sprinkle with pecans before serving, if desired. Makes 8 to 10 servings.

Molded gelatin salads were everywhere in the 1950's! Vintage molds can be found at flea markets...dress up a kitchen wall with a whimsical display.

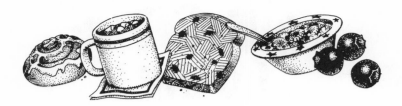

Berry Delicious Pie

Jennifer Cornish
Elmira, NY

This fresh fruit pie certainly lives up to its name!

3/4 c. sugar
3 T. cornstarch
1/8 t. salt
1/4 c. water
5 c. blueberries, divided

1 T. butter
1 T. lemon juice
9-inch pie crust, baked
Garnish: whipped topping

Heat sugar, cornstarch, salt and water in a saucepan until sugar dissolves, stirring until smooth. Add 3 cups blueberries; bring to a boil for 2 minutes, stirring constantly or until thickened and bubbly. Remove from heat; add butter, lemon juice and remaining blueberries. Stir until butter is melted; cool. Pour blueberry mixture into pie crust; refrigerate until serving. Serve with a dollop of whipped topping. Makes 8 servings.

Diners are famous for oh-so perfect pie crust. Their secret is using equal amounts of chilled butter and room-temperature shortening for a tender & flaky pastry every time!

LOBSTER LOUIE'S

Bar Harbor Cranberry Pie

Jean Hayes
La Porte, TX

*Frozen berries can also be used...no need to thaw
before preparing this pretty pie.*

2 c. cranberries
1-1/2 c. sugar, divided
1/2 c. chopped pecans
2 eggs, beaten

1 c. all-purpose flour
1/2 c. margarine, melted
1/4 c. shortening, melted

Lightly butter a 9" glass pie plate; spread cranberries over the bottom. Sprinkle evenly with 1/2 cup sugar and pecans; set aside. In a separate bowl, add eggs and remaining sugar; mix well. Blend in flour, margarine and shortening; beat well after each addition. Pour over cranberries; bake at 325 degrees for one hour. Serves 8.

The alternative to a vacation is to stay home
and tip every third person you see.
– Unknown

Vermont Raisin Cookies

Lisa Garrett
Williamsport, OH

Enjoy these nutty cookies with a tall glass of milk
or a cup of hot herbal tea.

1 c. water
2 c. raisins
1 c. shortening
1-3/4 c. sugar
2 eggs, beaten
1 t. vanilla extract
3-1/2 c. all-purpose flour

1 t. baking powder
1 t. baking soda
1 t. salt
1 T. cinnamon
1/2 t. nutmeg
1 c. chopped walnuts

Bring water and raisins to a boil in a small saucepan; boil for
3 minutes. Remove from heat; cool, do not drain. Cream shortening
and sugar in a large mixing bowl; add eggs and vanilla. In a separate
bowl, combine dry ingredients; gradually add to creamed mixture,
mixing thoroughly. Stir in nuts and raisin mixture; drop by
teaspoonfuls onto greased baking sheets. Bake at 350 degrees for
12 to 14 minutes. Makes about 6 dozen.

State route signs are unique landmarks that we pass along
the way and may not even notice! Look for vintage signs at
flea markets to remember road trips in a brand new way.

LOBSTER LOUIE'S

Cream Puff Cake

Susan Biffignani
Fenton, MO

This yummy cake looks like it takes a long time to prepare, but it's oh-so simple!

1 c. water
1/2 c. butter, softened
1 c. all-purpose flour
4 eggs
8-oz. pkg. cream cheese, softened

3 3.4-oz. boxes instant vanilla pudding
4 c. milk
8-oz. carton whipped topping
Garnish: chocolate syrup

Pour water into a saucepan; add butter. Bring to a boil; whisk in flour. Remove from heat; cool. Add eggs, one at a time, beating well after each addition; spread into a greased 13"x9" baking pan. Bake in a 400-degree oven for 30 to 35 minutes; cool. Combine cream cheese and one package of pudding mix together until smooth; add remaining pudding and milk. Pour over crust; let set 3 hours or overnight. Spread with whipped topping and drizzle with chocolate syrup before serving. Makes 12 to 15 servings.

Travel tip: Back seat giggles can help pass the time.

Why does a vacation in the mountains cost more than one at the seashore? Because everything is higher in the mountains.

What driver never needs a license? A screwdriver.

What do you call a pig that lives in the street? A road hog.

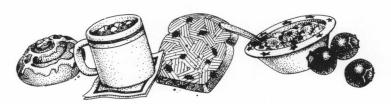

Double Maple Cupcakes

Gail Prather
Bethel, MN

*I love using the fresh maple syrup I get at our local farmers'
market for these cupcakes...it gives them such
a nice maple flavor.*

1/2 c. sugar
5 T. butter, softened
1 t. vanilla extract
1/2 t. maple flavoring
2 eggs

1-1/4 c. all-purpose flour
1-1/4 t. baking powder
1/4 t. salt
1/4 c. milk
1/4 c. maple syrup

Blend sugar, butter, vanilla and maple flavoring on medium speed
until well-blended. Add eggs, one at a time, blending well after each
addition; set aside. Sift flour, baking powder and salt together in a
mixing bowl; set aside. Combine milk and syrup together in a separate
mixing bowl. Add flour and syrup mixture alternately into sugar
mixture, beginning and ending with flour; mix well after each
addition. Spoon batter into 12 muffin cups lined with paper liners;
bake at 350 degrees for 20 minutes or until done. Cool in pan for
10 minutes; remove and cool completely on wire racks. Frost. Makes
12 cupcakes.

Frosting:

3 T. maple syrup
2 T. butter, softened
1/2 t. vanilla extract

1/2 t. maple flavoring
1/8 t. salt
1-3/4 c. powdered sugar

Blend first 5 ingredients together on medium speed of a mixer for one
minute; gradually blend in powdered sugar until smooth and creamy.

**When taking along snacks for the ride,
slice cupcakes in half, ice and put them back together
so that the icing is in the middle...neat & tidy!**

LIBERTY'S
Diner

Take a bite of the Big Apple.

Breakfast Scramble

Kathy Unruh
Fresno, CA

*This is a breakfast tradition in our family,
especially at Christmas and Easter.*

1/2 c. sliced mushrooms
1/4 c. onion, chopped
1/2 bunch spinach, chopped
6 slices bacon, crisply cooked
  and crumbled, drippings
  reserved

6 eggs
2 T. milk
1/8 t. pepper
1/4 c. shredded Monterey Jack
  cheese

Sauté mushrooms, onion and spinach in 2 tablespoons of reserved bacon drippings until tender; set aside. Whisk eggs, milk and pepper together; pour into skillet with spinach mixture. Heat over medium heat until eggs are almost set, about 3 minutes, stirring occasionally. Add bacon and cheese; heat until eggs are set. Makes 4 servings.

Wake-Up Shake

Elaine Goldberg
Ocean City, NJ

*Start your day with a taste reminiscent of those
childhood Creamsicles.*

1 c. milk
1 T. orange juice concentrate,
  unthawed

1 t. vanilla extract
sugar to taste
4 to 6 ice cubes

Pour ingredients into a blender; blend until smooth. Makes one serving.

**For a breakfast or lunch table, fill eggcups with
wildflowers and leave one at each place setting.**

LIBERTY'S
Diner

Mini Quiches

Kerrie Miller
Kerman, CA

*Use this recipe to make one large quiche too! Just add an egg, double
all other ingredients, pour into a pie crust and bake until set.*

2 9-inch refrigerated pie crusts,
   unbaked
2 eggs
1/2 c. milk
3/4 c. zucchini, chopped
1/2 c. mushrooms, chopped

1/2 c. shredded Cheddar cheese
1/4 c. cooked ham, diced
1/4 c. green onions, sliced
1 clove garlic, minced
salt and pepper to taste

Roll out each pie crust into a 12"x12" square on a lightly floured
surface; using a glass, cut each square into 12 circles. Press into
greased mini muffin pans; set aside. Whisk together eggs and milk in a
medium mixing bowl; stir in remaining ingredients. Spoon about one
tablespoon of filling into each muffin cup; bake at 375 degrees for
15 to 18 minutes or until puffed and golden. Cool in pan for 2 to
3 minutes; remove carefully and serve warm. Makes 2 dozen.

Life's a trip! May you wish upon a thousand stars, may you
catch a million fireflies. May you return home with loads of
pearly shells, pressed flowers and pink sand. And may you
realize just how much you learn when you look
at life through the eyes of a child.
— Unknown

Sunrise Ham

Kristi Stahl
Hutchinson, MN

Fresh fruit is a refreshing complement to this creamy dish.

1 c. cooked ham, diced
1 c. sliced mushrooms
1 T. margarine, melted
4 eggs
1 c. sour cream
1 c. cottage cheese
1/2 c. fresh Parmesan cheese,
    grated

1/4 c. all-purpose flour
1/2 t. dill weed
1/2 t. dry mustard
1/8 t. nutmeg
1/8 t. pepper
1 c. shredded Swiss cheese
1/2 c. fresh parsley, chopped

Cook ham in a skillet until slightly browned; set aside. Sauté mushrooms in margarine until tender; mix with ham and place in a greased 9" pie pan. Combine eggs, sour cream, cottage cheese, Parmesan cheese, flour, dill, mustard, nutmeg and pepper in a blender; blend until smooth. Stir in Swiss cheese and parsley; pour over ham and mushrooms. Bake at 350 degrees for 40 to 45 minutes; let stand 10 minutes before cutting. Makes 6 to 8 servings.

Greet each morning with a whimsical vintage juice glass.
Look for glasses splashed with polka dots, cherries,
circus animals or even Davy Crockett!

LIBERTY'S
Diner

Spinach & Bacon Quiche

Carolyn Baer
Whitehouse, TX

Hearty enough to be served any time of day!

10-oz. pkg. frozen chopped
    spinach, thawed and drained
4 eggs, beaten
1-1/2 c. half-and-half
1.8-oz. pkg. leek soup mix
1/4 t. pepper
10 slices bacon, crisply cooked
    and crumbled

1/2 c. shredded mozzarella
    cheese
1/2 c. shredded sharp Cheddar
    cheese
9-inch frozen pie crust, unbaked

Drain spinach between layers of paper towels; set aside. Whisk eggs, half-and-half, leek soup mix and pepper together in a medium mixing bowl; stir in spinach, bacon and cheeses. Pour into frozen pie crust; place on a baking sheet and bake at 375 degrees for 40 to 45 minutes. Makes 8 servings.

Most diners still serve breakfast 24 hours a day...discover the fun of having a bottomless cup of coffee and a western omelet for dinner.

Mushroom & Steak Hoagies

Mandy Sheets
Homedale, ID

Soy sauce lends a unique taste to this delicious steak sandwich.

1 c. water
1/3 c. soy sauce
1-1/2 t. garlic powder
1-1/2 t. pepper
1-lb. round steak, cut into
  1/4-inch strips

1 onion, chopped
1 green pepper, thinly sliced
4-oz. can mushroom stems and
  pieces, drained
2 c. shredded mozzarella cheese
6 hoagie buns, split

Whisk water, soy sauce, garlic powder and pepper together; add steak, turning to coat. Cover and refrigerate overnight. Drain and discard marinade; brown steak in a large skillet. Add onion, green pepper and mushrooms; sauté until tender. Reduce heat; top with cheese. Remove from heat; stir until cheese melts and meat is coated. Spoon onto buns to serve. Makes 6.

Onion Rings

Jo Ann

Crispy and delicious with just a hint of sweetness!

3 sweet onions, thickly sliced
  and separated into rings
1-1/2 t. baking powder
1 c. all-purpose flour
1 t. salt

1 egg
2/3 c. water
1/2 T. lemon juice
1 T. butter, melted
oil for deep-frying

Soak onion rings in ice water for 1/2 hour; pat dry with paper towels and set aside. Sift baking powder, flour and salt together; set aside. Combine egg, water and lemon juice; beat well. Stir into flour mixture until just blended; add butter. Dip onion rings into batter; drop into 375 degree oil and fry 2 minutes on each side. Drain. Serves 6.

LIBERTY'S
Diner

White Chicken Pizza

Michelle Schuberg
Big Rapids, MI

A quick & easy dinner even your most finicky eater will love!

10-oz. can refrigerated pizza
   dough
2 boneless skinless chicken
   breasts
2 T. minced garlic
1 T. olive oil

16-oz. jar Alfredo sauce
1/4 c. onion, chopped
8-oz. pkg. shredded mozzarella,
   Parmesan & Romano cheese
   blend

Spread dough onto a lightly greased round pizza baking pan; bake at 425 degrees for 7 minutes. While baking, cube chicken; sauté with garlic in oil until juices run clear when pierced with a fork. Pour Alfredo sauce over baked crust; sprinkle with chicken and onion. Bake 10 more minutes; top with cheese blend and return to oven until cheeses melt. Makes 8 servings.

What a clever way to serve a sandwich and chips for lunch...look for jaunty red baskets at restaurant or kitchen supply stores, line with wax paper and serve in diner-style!

International Hero

Paula Hanna
Lubbock, TX

*Keeps fresh in the fridge for several days
and is perfect for family picnics.*

1 loaf French bread
4 T. butter, softened
2 T. garlic spread, softened
1/2 c. sweet pickle relish
14-oz. can sauerkraut, drained

1/2 lb. sliced ham
1/2 lb. sliced Genoa salami
1/4 lb. sliced pepperoni
1/4 lb. sliced Swiss cheese
1/4 lb. sliced American cheese

Slice French bread loaf in half horizontally; spread butter on top and bottom slices. Spread garlic, relish and sauerkraut on top layer only; stack meat and cheese slices on bottom half. Replace the top half; slice into 2-inch thick servings. Makes 4 servings.

Cheese Fries

Wendy Lee Paffenroth
Pine Island, NY

Dip in sour cream or ranch dressing.

32-oz. pkg. frozen French fries
1/2 c. green onions, sliced
1/2 c. bacon, crisply cooked and
    crumbled

2 T. chili powder
1 c. shredded Cheddar cheese

Bake French fries according to package directions; place in a broiler pan. Sprinkle with chili powder, onion, bacon and cheese; broil for about 2 minutes or until cheese is melted. Makes 8 servings.

Become the "Auto Santa" on your next trip. Wrap up a little gift to hand out to each child at every pit stop. It will make the miles fly by for little ones!

LIBERTY'S
Diner

Creamy Italian Sub

Leslie Stimel
Gooseberry Patch

*No time for dinner? Pack these in a cooler and take them
along to the ballpark in plenty of time for the game.*

1/2 c. mayonnaise-type salad
    dressing
1/4 c. Italian salad dressing
3 c. shredded lettuce
4 6-inch French bread rolls,
    split

10-oz. pkg. sliced ham
10-oz. pkg. sliced salami
8 slices hot pepper cheese
1 tomato, thinly sliced
1 green pepper, thinly sliced

Mix mayonnaise-type salad dressing and Italian dressing together;
toss 1/4 cup of mayonnaise mix with lettuce and set aside. Brush rolls
with remaining salad dressing; layer meats, cheese, tomato, green
pepper and lettuce mixture on bottom of each roll. Replace tops.
Makes 4 sandwiches.

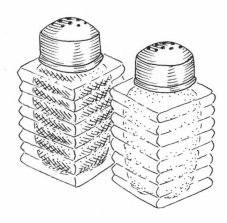

Look for mismatched salt & pepper shakers. They add charm
to your table and everyone can have their own set.

Beef Stroganoff Sandwich

Linda Hendrix
Moundville, MO

*Broil the bread before adding on ingredients
for an extra tasty treat!*

2 lbs. ground beef
1/2 c. onion, chopped
1 t. salt
1/2 t. garlic powder
1/4 t. pepper
1 loaf French bread

4 T. margarine
2 16-oz. cartons sour cream
2 tomatoes, sliced
1 green pepper, sliced
3 c. shredded Cheddar cheese

Brown ground beef and onion; drain. Add salt, garlic powder and pepper; set aside. Cut bread in half horizontally; butter both sides and place on baking sheets. Stir sour cream into meat mixture; spoon onto bread. Layer tomatoes and green peppers over the top. Bake at 350 degrees for 10 minutes; remove from oven and sprinkle with cheese. Bake 10 more minutes or until cheese is melted. Makes 6 to 8 servings.

There's music to play, places to go, people to see...
everything for you and me!
– Lee Adams

LIBERTY'S
Diner

Fried Potato Chowder

Kristie Rigo
Friedens, PA

The fried potatoes in this soup give it a new twist.

1 lb. bacon
6 potatoes, diced
1 onion, diced
1 carrot, peeled and grated
4 c. milk

10-3/4 oz. can cream of chicken
 soup
15-1/4 oz. can corn, drained
salt and pepper to taste

Cut bacon into one-inch slices and heat until crisp; do not drain. Add potatoes, onion and carrots; heat until potatoes are tender, stirring occasionally. Stir in milk, soup, corn, salt and pepper; simmer for 15 minutes. Makes 6 to 8 servings.

Retro diner signs make a great backdrop for candid snapshots...you'll never forget those crispy onion rings or the great conversation when the diner is right there in your photos!

Chicken & Spinach Calzones

Jennifer Smith
Manchester, CT

A great recipe using pre-made dough...what a time-saver!

2 boneless skinless chicken
   breasts, cubed
1/4 c. onion, chopped
1 c. frozen chopped spinach,
   cooked and drained
2 t. dried basil

3/4 c. pizza sauce
1/2 c. ricotta cheese
3 oz. mozzarella cheese, cubed
10-oz. can refrigerated pizza
   dough

Sauté chicken until juices run clear when pierced with a fork; add onion and sauté 2 minutes. Reduce heat; add spinach, basil, pizza sauce and ricotta cheese. Remove from heat; stir in mozzarella cheese and set aside. Divide pizza dough into 4 equal pieces; roll each piece into a 6-inch circle. Spoon equal amounts chicken and spinach mixture into each circle; fold dough in half. Seal edges with a fork; set on lightly greased baking sheet. Bake at 425 degrees for 15 minutes or until crust is golden brown. Makes 4 servings.

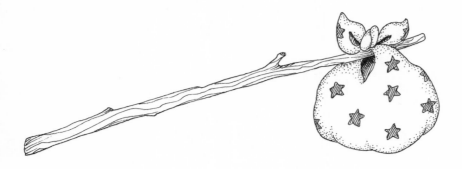

Surprise the family with a hobo lunch! Wrap a sandwich, candy bar and a piece of fruit in a bandanna and tie it to a stick...fun for a hike!

LIBERTY'S
Diner

3-Cheese Bruschetta

Vickie

A light and tasty appetizer with Italian flair.

12-inch ready-to-eat pizza crust
2 T. butter, melted
3 cloves garlic, minced
2 t. dried basil
5 plum tomatoes, thinly sliced
garlic salt and pepper to taste

1 c. shredded mozzarella cheese
1 c. shredded sharp Cheddar cheese
1/2 c. fresh Parmesan cheese, grated

Brush pizza crust with butter; sprinkle with garlic and basil. Arrange tomato slices over the pizza; add garlic salt and pepper to taste. Top with cheeses; place on a baking sheet. Bake at 400 degrees for 8 to 10 minutes or until cheeses melt; serve hot. Makes 6 servings.

Keep a travel journal. It can hold memories you may otherwise forget...anything from funny signs, great meals or what you see out the car window.

Reuben Casserole

Vicki Knapp
Akron, OH

*Serve a garden-fresh salad with this
deli sandwich-turned-casserole.*

1 c. sour cream
1 c. sauerkraut, rinsed and
   drained
1 lb. corned beef, thinly sliced

2 c. shredded Swiss cheese
10 slices rye bread, cubed
1/2 c. butter, melted

Combine sour cream and drained sauerkraut together; spread in
bottom of 13"x9" baking pan. Layer corned beef, cheese and then rye
bread; pour melted butter over the top. Bake, covered, at 350 degrees
for 30 minutes; bake uncovered an additional 15 minutes. Makes
12 servings.

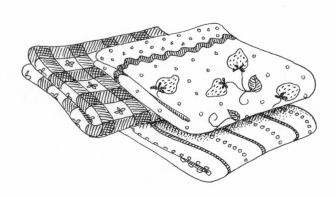

Until you decide how to use your stash of vintage kitchen
linens and feedsacks, show them off! Stack them up on a
pantry shelf, in a wire basket or hang from an
old-fashioned drying rack.

LIBERTY'S
Diner

Herb Bagel Chips

Liz Plotnick-Snay
Gooseberry Patch

These crunchy minis are yummy alongside any dip.

1-1/2 t. Italian seasoning
1/4 t. onion powder
1/4 t. garlic powder
1/8 t. red pepper

9 frozen mini bagels, thawed
butter-flavored vegetable
   cooking spray

Combine spices in a jar with a shaker lid; set aside. Slice each bagel horizontally into 4 slices; place in a single layer on a lightly greased baking sheet. Lightly coat tops with cooking spray; sprinkle with spice mix. Bake at 375 degrees for 12 minutes or until crisp. Makes 3 dozen.

Bagel Dip

Judie Gretz
Coopersburg, PA

Spread on bagels, pitas or sourdough.

10-3/4 oz. can cream of mushroom soup
8-oz. pkg. cream cheese,
   softened

1/4 lb. pepperoni, chopped

Mix soup and cream cheese together until smooth; stir in pepperoni. Place in a small oven-proof baking dish; bake at 350 degrees for 30 minutes. Serve warm. Makes about 2 cups.

**If this is coffee, then please bring me some tea but
if this is tea then please bring me some coffee!
– Abraham Lincoln**

Squash & Pepper Bake

Dale Driggers
Lexington, SC

Just like chili, it's even better the second day.

4 to 5 yellow squash, thinly
   sliced
1 onion, thinly sliced
1 green pepper, thinly sliced
4 tomatoes, peeled and chopped

2 t. salt
1/2 t. pepper
3 T. long-cooking rice, uncooked
2 T. brown sugar, packed
1 T. butter

Combine all ingredients, except brown sugar and butter; place in a 1-1/2 quart greased casserole dish. Sprinkle with brown sugar; dot with butter. Bake, covered, at 350 degrees for 45 minutes or until vegetables are tender, stirring halfway through baking time. Let stand 10 minutes before serving. Serves 8.

Stop worrying about the potholes in the road
and celebrate the journey!
– Fitzhugh Mullan

LIBERTY'S
Diner

Heavenly Potatoes

Camille Jones
Suwanee, GA

Easy to make and SO scrumptious!

1 onion, finely chopped
2 T. butter
24-oz. pkg. frozen shredded
   hash browns, thawed
2 c. sharp Cheddar cheese,
   grated

10-3/4 oz. can cream of chicken
   soup
2 c. sour cream
salt and pepper to taste

Sauté onion in butter until tender; combine with remaining ingredients. Pour into a 2-quart casserole dish; bake at 350 degrees for one hour. Makes 8 to 10 servings.

Next time you're out on a day trip try to stop by a few garage sales or the local flea market. Keep an eye out for vintage toys...a one-of-a-kind to surprise a little one at home.

Stuffed Shells

Melle Bain
Waco, TX

Any extra prep time is worth it for the rave reviews!

2 lbs. ground beef
3 cloves garlic, minced
Italian seasoning to taste
salt and pepper to taste
2 16-oz. jars spaghetti sauce,
    divided

1 c. shredded mozzarella cheese,
    divided
12-oz. pkg. jumbo pasta shells,
    cooked and drained

Brown ground beef with garlic, Italian seasonings, salt and pepper; drain. Stir in 1/2 jar spaghetti sauce and 1/2 cup cheese into meat mixture; spoon into shells and set aside. Pour 1/2 jar spaghetti sauce into the bottom of a 13"x9" baking pan; add shells. Pour remaining jar of spaghetti sauce over shells; sprinkle with remaining cheese. Bake, uncovered, at 350 degrees for 30 to 40 minutes. Serves 6 to 8.

The simplest toy even
the youngest child
can operate is called
a grandparent.
– Sam Levenson

LIBERTY'S
Diner

Spinach Casserole

Sue Bogumil
West Seneca, NY

*This reliable side dish goes with anything
and couldn't be easier.*

2 c. cottage cheese
3 eggs, beaten
3 T. all-purpose flour
1/4 lb. Colby Jack cheese, cubed

10-oz. pkg. frozen spinach,
  partially thawed
2 T. butter
1/8 t. salt

Combine cottage cheese, eggs and flour together; mix well. Stir in Colby Jack cheese and spinach; add butter and salt. Pour into a 2-quart baking dish; bake, uncovered, at 350 degrees for one hour. Makes 6 servings.

Tape a large envelope to the outside of the telephone book...perfect for holding take-out menus and coupons.

Chicken Paprikash

Kate Conroy
Bethlehem, PA

*This is an old recipe handed down by my father's family
and is rich in Hungarian tradition.*

1 to 1-1/2 lbs. boneless skinless
  chicken breasts, chopped
1/4 c. butter
1 onion, sliced
1/4 c. water
1 cube chicken bouillon

1 T. paprika
1 t. salt
1/8 t. pepper
1 c. sour cream
12-oz. pkg. butter noodles,
  cooked and drained

Brown chicken in butter in a large skillet over medium heat; add
onion and cook for 5 minutes. Mix in remaining ingredients except
for the sour cream and noodles; bring to a boil. Reduce heat; simmer,
covered, for 30 minutes, stirring occasionally. Add sour cream when
juices of chicken run clear when pierced with a fork. Heat thoroughly
without bringing to a boil; pour chicken and sauce over noodles.
Serves 4 to 6.

**Daydream and take a mini vacation the next time you see a
jet's vapor trail. Pretend you're going along for the ride!**

LIBERTY'S
Diner

Chicken Cordon Bleu

Glenda Tebbens
Lincoln, DE

Try to find the largest chicken breasts you can...makes them so much easier to roll!

5 boneless skinless chicken
   breasts, pounded thin
salt and pepper to taste
1 T. fresh chives, chopped
10 thin slices cooked ham

10 slices American cheese
10 slices bacon
10-3/4 oz. can cream of mushroom soup
1 c. whipping cream

Salt and pepper each chicken breast; sprinkle with chives. Place
2 slices of ham and 2 slices of cheese on each chicken breast; roll up
each breast. Wrap 2 slices of bacon around each roll; secure with
toothpicks. Place in a lightly greased 13"x9" baking dish; bake at
350 degrees for 45 minutes. Heat mushroom soup and cream in a
heavy saucepan over medium heat until smooth and heated through,
stirring constantly. Ladle over chicken breasts to serve. Makes
5 servings.

String a clothesline under a cabinet and hang potholders with
mini clothespins...collect colors and designs
to match your kitchen.

Caramelized Onion Jam

Gail Prather
Bethel, MN

*Onions will be sweet with a smoky flavor and
have a lovely caramel brown color when done.*

8 c. onions, thinly sliced
1/4 c. brown sugar, packed
1 T. red wine vinegar

4 T. butter, sliced
1 T. honey

Place onions in a large saucepan; sprinkle with brown sugar and vinegar. Dot with butter; drizzle with honey. Cover; cook over medium heat until onions are tender, about 15 minutes. Uncover; raise heat to high and cook until onions are browned and caramelized, about 10 minutes. Serve warm; store, covered, in refrigerator for up to one week. Makes 2 cups.

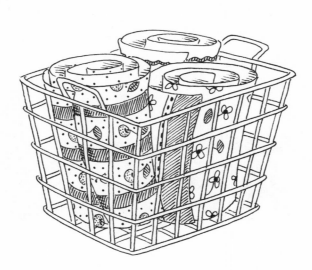

**Vintage wire containers like locker and market baskets make
perfect catch-alls for extra dishtowels.**

LIBERTY'S
Diner

Parmesan–Sage Pork Chops

Ann Keebaugh
Herndon, VA

These chops turn out so moist and have a heavenly flavor.

1-1/2 c. bread crumbs
1 c. fresh Parmesan cheese,
   grated
1 T. dried sage
1 t. lemon zest
2 eggs
1/4 c. all-purpose flour

salt and pepper to taste
4 pork chops
2 T. butter, melted
2 T. olive oil
Garnish: lemon and orange
   slices

Toss bread crumbs, cheese, sage and lemon zest together; set aside.
Whisk eggs together in a shallow bowl; set aside. Place flour on a
plate; season with salt and pepper. Coat pork chops with flour; dip
into eggs then coat with bread crumb mixture. Pour butter and oil
in a large oven-proof skillet; add pork chops. Brown about 2 minutes
on each side; transfer skillet to oven. Bake at 425 degrees for
20 minutes or until a meat thermometer inserted into a pork chop
registers 150 degrees. Garnish with lemon and orange wedges.
Makes 4 servings.

**Collect charms to create a special keepsake of your travels...it's
like wearing a mini-scrapbook around your wrist!**

Cheesy Corn Chowder

Linda Davidson
Grove City, OH

This recipe is a quick & easy way to make
toasty soup for hungry family or friends.

1 onion, chopped
2 stalks celery, chopped
4 T. butter
2 15-oz. cans creamed corn
6 potatoes, chopped and boiled

4 c. chicken broth
3 c. milk
1/2 c. shredded Colby cheese
6 slices bacon, crisply cooked
   and crumbled

Sauté onion and celery in butter until tender; add corn, heating thoroughly. Pour into a Dutch oven; stir in potatoes, chicken broth, milk and cheese. Heat over medium heat until cheese melts; do not boil. Stir in bacon. Makes 6 to 8 servings.

Lose a sock on vacation? Use those lonely single socks to make sock puppets...yarn, felt scraps and even old buttons are a great way to decorate them!

LIBERTY'S
Diner

Chicken Pie Roll-Ups

Janet Henriksen
Kingsburg, CA

Double the batch...these appetizers go fast!

8-oz. can refrigerated crescent
   rolls
3-oz. pkg. cream cheese,
   softened
2 T. plus 1/8 t. butter, melted
   and divided
2 c. chicken breasts, cooked and
   diced

2 T. milk
1 T. onion, chopped
1 T. pimento
1/4 t. salt
1/8 t. pepper
1/2 c. croutons, crushed

Prepare pastry by pushing seams together on two crescent rolls, making 4 rolls per one can of crescent rolls; set aside. Blend cream cheese and 2 tablespoons melted butter together; add chicken, milk, onion, pimento, salt and pepper, mixing well. Spoon mixture into center of each pastry; pull up corners and pinch pastry closed. Brush with remaining butter; sprinkle with croutons. Bake on an ungreased baking sheet at 350 degrees for 20 to 25 minutes. Makes 4 servings.

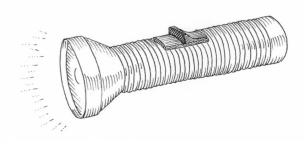

Play a game of flashlight tag in the twilight this summer.
Whoever is "it" must shine their light on others to tag
them...what fun to scamper in the grass like kids again!

Chicken Blues

Heather Heald-Leighton
Farmingdale, ME

Tasty hot or cold!

2 c. bread crumbs
1/2 t. celery salt
1/4 t. dill weed
salt and pepper to taste

8-oz. bottle blue cheese dressing
6 to 8 boneless skinless chicken
breasts

Toss bread crumbs, celery salt, dill, salt and pepper together; set aside.
Pour dressing into a shallow pan; coat chicken with dressing then roll
in crumb mixture. Bake chicken in a greased 13"x9" baking pan at
350 degrees for one hour or until juices run clear when pierced with a
fork. Makes 6 to 8 servings.

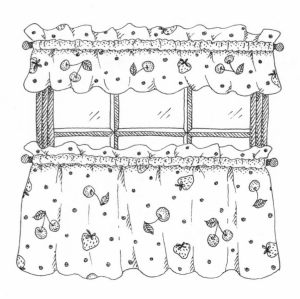

Make a café curtain and valance out of a
vintage tablecloth in a cheery 1950's print.

LIBERTY'S
Diner

Rosemary Twists

*Gail Prather
Lakeside, CA*

Scrumptious when served with savory soups and stews.

1/3 c. butter, melted
1 t. dried rosemary
1/2 t. garlic, minced
2-1/4 c. all-purpose flour

2 T. grated Parmesan cheese
1 T. sugar
3-1/2 t. baking powder
1 c. milk

Pour butter, rosemary and garlic into a 13"x9" baking pan; tilt to coat bottom of pan. Combine flour, cheese, sugar and baking powder in a mixing bowl; stir in milk until just moistened. Turn dough onto a lightly floured surface; knead 10 times or until smooth. Roll dough into a 12"x6" rectangle; cut into 12, one-inch strips. Twist each strip about 6 times; lay in baking pan and roll to coat with butter mixture. Bake at 400 degrees for 20 to 25 minutes or until lightly browned. Makes 12.

Have you ever seen an elephant in the clouds? Be a kid again for just an afternoon...take some time to lie on your back in the grass and watch the clouds drift by.

Chocolate Cheesecake

Sheryl Kramer
Oshkosh, WI

Easy to make and best of all, it requires NO baking!

16-oz. box honey graham
  crackers, finely crushed
1 c. dry roasted peanuts,
  chopped
1/2 c. butter, melted
8-oz. pkg. cream cheese,
  softened

1 c. powdered sugar
16-oz. container whipped
  topping
2 4-oz. pkgs. chocolate instant
  pudding
3 c. milk
1-1/2 toffee candy bars, chopped

Combine graham cracker crumbs, peanuts and butter; spread in a
13"x9" baking pan and set aside. Blend cream cheese, powdered sugar
and 2 cups whipped topping together; spread over crust. Blend
chocolate pudding and milk together about 2 minutes; pour over
cream cheese layer. Top with remaining whipped topping; sprinkle
with toffee candy bar. Refrigerate until set. Makes 15 servings.

You can find your way across this
country using burger joints the way a
navigator uses stars. We have
munched Bridge
burgers in the
shadow of the
Brooklyn Bridge
and Dixie burgers in
the deep South!
– Charles Kuralt

LIBERTY'S
Diner

Creamy Cheesecake

Marsha Eunice
Jefferson, OR

This recipe was given to me by my grandmother in 1961 and has remained a family favorite after all these years.

20 graham crackers, finely
   crushed
1/4 c. butter, softened
1 c. plus 3 T. sugar, divided
4 eggs, beaten
3 8-oz. pkgs. cream cheese,
   softened

1 c. sour cream
1/2 t. vanilla extract
1/8 t. lemon juice
1/8 t. salt

Mix graham cracker crumbs, butter and 2 tablespoons sugar together; press into the bottom and 2 inches up the sides of a 9" springform pan. In a separate mixing bowl, blend eggs, cream cheese and one cup sugar. Pour into crust; bake at 350 degrees for 20 minutes. Remove from oven; set on cooling rack. Cool 20 minutes. Combine sour cream, remaining sugar, vanilla, lemon juice and salt; mix well. Gently spoon over top of cheesecake; bake at 450 degrees for 5 minutes. Cool; refrigerate overnight. Makes 10 servings.

"Bottomless" Cup COFFEE 20¢

When visiting New York, don't miss Jones Beach State Park. Back when it opened in the 1930's, the whole park had a cruise ship theme...how fun!

Peppered Rib Eye Steaks

Jo Ann

*A special presentation for company and
simple enough for every day.*

4 rib eye steaks
2 T. olive oil
1 clove garlic, minced
1 T. garlic powder
1 T. paprika
2 t. dried thyme

2 t. dried oregano
1-1/2 t. pepper
1 t. salt
1 t. lemon pepper
1 t. cayenne pepper

Brush steaks lightly with olive oil and garlic; combine remaining
ingredients; coat steaks. Cover and chill for one hour. Grill steaks to
desired doneness; cut across grain into thick slices. Makes 8 servings.

To decorate a small wall space, use vintage red or
green-handled utensils or cookie cutters. Simply
hang them on tacks, cup hooks or pegs!

LIBERTY'S
Diner

Garden Eggplant

Susan Biffignani
Fenton, MO

*My mother-in-law shared this recipe with me. I made it the first time
I cooked for her son, my soon-to-be husband.*

1 eggplant, sliced
salt to taste
2 T. oil

1 onion, diced
14-1/2 oz. can whole tomatoes
1/8 t. sugar

Salt eggplant to taste; sauté in oil until tender. Remove eggplant to
a paper towel; reserve oil. Sauté onion in reserved oil; add tomatoes
and sugar. Heat thoroughly. Layer eggplant and tomato mixture into
a 1-1/2 quart microwave-safe casserole dish; heat on high in the
microwave for 10 minutes. Serve warm. Makes 4 servings.

**Matching range sets were on every stove in the 1950's.
Keep an eye out for a jadite or colored glass set and
add vintage charm to your kitchen!**

Broadway Brownie Bars

Beth Ondrejovic
Jefferson, OH

Rich, decadent and always a hit!

1 c. cream cheese, divided
1-1/2 c. sugar, divided
1 c. plus 2 T. all-purpose flour,
    divided
1 c. butter, softened and divided
3 eggs, divided
2-1/2 t. vanilla extract, divided
2 sqs. unsweetened chocolate,
    divided

1-1/4 c. chopped walnuts,
    divided
1 t. baking powder
1 c. semi-sweet chocolate chips
2 c. mini marshmallows
4 c. milk
3 c. powdered sugar

Blend 3/4 cup cream cheese, 1/2 cup sugar, 2 tablespoons flour, 1/4 cup butter, one egg and 1/2 teaspoon vanilla together; set aside. Melt one square chocolate and 1/2 cup butter in a saucepan over medium heat; remove from heat. Stir in one cup sugar, one cup flour, one cup nuts, baking powder, one teaspoon vanilla and remaining eggs; mix well. Pour into a lightly greased 13"x9" pan; spread cream cheese mixture on top. Toss together 1/4 cup nuts and chocolate chips; sprinkle over cream cheese layer. Bake at 350 degrees for 28 minutes; scatter marshmallows on top and return to oven for 2 more minutes. Melt remaining butter, chocolate, cream cheese and milk in a saucepan, stirring often; remove from heat. Stir in powdered sugar and remaining vanilla; immediately drizzle over marshmallows. Chill; cut into bars. Makes 30 bars.

Give old fabrics a brand new role! Cheery prints from the 1950's make eye-catching wallhangings when framed. Paint the frame to accent a favorite color in the fabric.

LIBERTY'S
Diner

Wake-Up Scones

Mary Murray
Gooseberry Patch

With coffee, tea or even cocoa, you'll love 'em!

1-3/4 c. all-purpose flour
1/3 c. gingersnap cookies,
   crushed
1/4 c. sugar
1-1/2 t. baking powder
1/2 t. baking soda

1/4 t. salt
1/4 c. cold butter, sliced
1/2 c. buttermilk
1 egg, beaten
10 walnut halves

Combine first six ingredients together; cut in butter until mixture resembles coarse crumbs. Add buttermilk and egg; stir until just moistened. Turn dough onto a lightly floured surface; knead lightly 4 times. Pat dough into a 10-inch circle on a lightly greased baking sheet; score into 10 wedges. Bake at 400 degrees for 15 minutes or until golden. Drizzle scones with espresso glaze; cut into 10 wedges and top each with a walnut half. Makes 10 servings.

Espresso Glaze:

1 T. hot water
2 t. instant coffee granules

1 c. powdered sugar

Combine hot water and coffee granules in a medium mixing bowl; stir until coffee dissolves. Add powdered sugar; mix until creamy.

There's always a place at the fire for a new friend, a spot on the grill for another steak and space in your kid's tummy for another s'more.
-Unknown

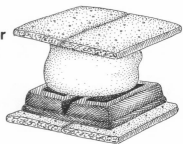

Orange-Macadamia Biscotti

Donna Rosser
Fayetteville, GA

I won first place in the baking division of the
Orange Blossom Recipe Contest with this recipe.

1/2 c. butter, softened
3/4 c. sugar
2 eggs, beaten
juice and zest of one orange
1/2 t. cinnamon

1/4 t. salt
2 t. baking powder
3 c. all-purpose flour
3/4 c. chopped Macadamia nuts,
    toasted

Cream butter and sugar together; add eggs. Blend in orange juice and zest; set aside. Combine dry ingredients in another bowl; gradually add into sugar mixture. Fold in nuts; mix well. Turn dough onto a well-floured surface; with floured hands, shape dough into 2 balls. Place one ball on an ungreased baking sheet; pinch and pat dough into a log the length of the baking sheet. Repeat with remaining dough. Bake at 325 degrees for 20 minutes; remove and cool for 5 minutes. Slice logs into 3/4-inch slices at a 45-degree angle. Place slices cut side up onto baking sheet; return to oven for 10 minutes. Flip slices; bake another 10 minutes. Cool on a wire rack. Makes about 2-1/2 dozen.

Before you hit the road with the family, cut cookie bars, brownies, crispy rice treats or fudge into individual servings at home. Place ooey-gooey treats in colorful wax paper bags to hand out later...no more sticky fingers!

LIBERTY'S
Diner

Creamy Mocha Fudge

Lynda McCormick
Burkburnett, TX

This fudge is so special that I often give it as a Christmas gift...the hint of coffee mixed with rich chocolate makes it irresistible.

16-oz. bag semi-sweet chocolate chips
1 T. instant espresso coffee granules

14-oz. can sweetened condensed milk

Melt chocolate in double boiler; remove from heat and quickly stir in coffee. Add milk; stir until well blended. Pour into a lightly buttered 8"x8" pan; refrigerate until firm. Makes 2 dozen.

Home Run Bars

April Jones
Greer, SC

Quick, easy and delicious...these are a grand slam!

4 c. quick-cooking oats, uncooked
1 c. brown sugar, packed
1/4 c. corn syrup
1 c. peanut butter, divided

1 t. vanilla extract
3/4 c. butter, softened
2/3 c. chocolate chips
1/3 c. butterscotch chips

Combine oats, brown sugar, corn syrup, 1/3 cup peanut butter, vanilla and butter; spread in a greased 13"x9" baking pan. Bake at 400 degrees for 12 minutes. Stir chocolate chips, butterscotch chips and remaining peanut butter together; spread over hot bars. Makes 2 dozen.

Play a game of "Think Backs" on your next road trip. Someone suggests a letter and everyone thinks back to all the sights that were seen beginning with that letter.

Raspberry Bars

Barbara Stauffer
Bainbridge, OH

*Whip up these fruity treats for a potluck
and watch them disappear!*

1-1/4 c. all-purpose flour	1/2 c. shortening
1/2 c. sugar	1/2 c. seedless raspberry jam

Combine flour and sugar; cut in shortening until mixture resembles coarse crumbs. Press into a greased 9"x9" baking dish; bake at 350 degrees for 20 to 25 minutes. Spread with jam; top with crumb topping. Bake 15 to 20 minutes longer. Cool; cut into bars. Makes 1-1/2 dozen.

Crumb Topping:

2/3 c. all-purpose flour	1/2 c. chopped pecans
6 T. shortening	1/2 t. vanilla extract
6 T. sugar	

Mix ingredients together with a fork until it resembles coarse crumbs.

Next time you give a souvenir gift, use a map of the destination! Decorate the package with seashells, pine cones or even stickers that you've picked up along the way.

BEEFY STU'S

Heaping helpings from the heartland.

Puffy Oven Pancake

Corinne Ficek
Normal, IL

We love these served with warm maple syrup, fresh fruit or jam.

5 eggs
2 c. milk
1 c. all-purpose flour
3/4 t. salt

1 T. sugar
1 t. vanilla extract
3 T. butter, melted

Blend eggs in a blender until frothy; gradually pour in milk, blending well. Add flour, salt, sugar and vanilla, mixing well. Refrigerate mixture overnight. Coat bottom of a glass 13"x9" baking dish with melted butter; pour excess butter back into refrigerated mixture. Blend refrigerated mixture again; pour into baking dish. Bake at 425 degrees for 35 to 40 minutes. Makes 12 servings.

Mix pancake or waffle batter in a wide-mouth, spouted pitcher, then pour right onto the griddle...less dishes to wash!

BEEFY
STU'S

Sunny Granola

Karen Parsons
Burden, KS

Add dried fruits like cranberries or dates to cooled mixture for a different taste.

3 c. quick-cooking oats,
   uncooked
1/2 c. flaked coconut
1/2 c. sunflower seeds
1/4 c. nuts

1/2 c. peanut butter
1/2 c. honey
1/4 c. canola oil

Toss together dry ingredients; set aside. Combine peanut butter, honey and canola oil in a saucepan; heat until smooth, stirring often. Pour over dry ingredients; bake at 250 degrees for one hour, stirring every 15 minutes. Makes 5 to 6 cups.

Quick Energy Pick-Ups

Dena Lenneman
St. Cloud, MN

The kids can help make this tasty treat, but make plenty...they won't last long!

4 sqs. graham crackers, crushed
1 c. powdered sugar
1 c. crunchy peanut butter
1 c. mini chocolate chips

1/2 c. powdered milk
3 T. water
2/3 c. flaked coconut

Combine ingredients together in a bowl; shape into one-inch balls. Refrigerate until firm, about 20 minutes. Makes about 2 dozen.

When traveling in the car, take along reusable stickers for great entertainment...kids can stick and restick them on the window.

Breakfast Potato Pie

Cathleen Fini
Chester, NY

*Gather the family together for a hearty
breakfast...a great way to start the day!*

4 potatoes, peeled and cubed
2 9-inch pie crusts, unbaked
1 c. shredded Cheddar cheese

1 c. cooked ham, cubed
5 eggs, beaten
salt and pepper to taste

Boil potatoes until tender, about 20 minutes; drain. Spread potatoes
in pie crust; sprinkle with cheese and ham. Pour eggs over mixture;
season with salt and pepper. Cover with top pie crust; bake at
350 degrees for 45 minutes or until set. Makes 8 servings.

If you don't know where you're going, you can never get lost.
– Herb Cohen

BEEFY STU'S

Oven Omelet

Kathy Grashoff
Fort Wayne, IN

Whip up this simple but delicious omelet for a
quick breakfast favorite.

1/4 c. margarine, melted	1 c. milk
18 eggs	2 t. salt
1 c. sour cream	1/4 c. green onions, chopped

Pour margarine in a 13"x9" baking dish; tilt to coat bottom of dish. Beat eggs, sour cream, milk and salt until blended; stir in onions. Pour mixture into dish; bake at 325 degrees until eggs are set but still moist, about 35 minutes. Cut into squares. Makes 12 to 15 servings.

Popeye Egg

Beverly Mock
Pensacola, FL

Use seasonal cookie cutters to slice the bread
for an egg-stra special breakfast year 'round!

4 T. butter, softened	6 eggs
6 slices bread	

Butter both sides of each bread slice; cut out a 2-inch circle from center of each slice. Add bread to a greased skillet; break egg into center of bread. Cook about 2 minutes; flip bread and egg, cook until desired doneness. Repeat with remaining bread and eggs. Makes 6 servings.

Have fun with diner lingo at breakfast! Order up an "Adam & Eve on a raft" which is two poached eggs on toast or try your eggs "wrecked" or scrambled.

Old-Fashioned Meat Loaf

Karen Fritts
Erie, PA

Serve this hearty meat loaf with some
creamy mashed potatoes and corn.

3 slices bread, cubed
1 c. milk
1-1/2 lbs. ground beef
1/4 t. dried sage
1/2 t. salt
1/4 t. pepper

1 egg
1 clove garlic, minced
1 onion, minced
1 T. Worcestershire sauce
1/2 c. barbecue sauce

Toss bread with milk; add remaining ingredients except barbecue sauce, mixing well. Pat into a loaf on a lightly greased baking sheet; top with barbecue sauce. Bake at 350 degrees for 1-1/2 hours or until done. Makes 8 servings.

Capture the nostalgia of yesterday's kitchen. Search auctions and flea markets for vintage enamelware, brightly colored depression glass and blue, white and jade green milk glass. Keep an eye out for picnic tins and wire egg baskets too!

BEEFY
STU'S

Double-Cheese Scalloped Potatoes

Rogene Rogers
Bemidji, MN

Two kinds of cheese make these potatoes a treat!

5 c. potatoes, peeled, cooked and
  sliced
2 c. small curd cottage cheese
1-1/2 c. sour cream

1/2 c. onion, chopped
1/2 t. salt
1/2 t. garlic salt
1 c. shredded Cheddar cheese

Mix all ingredients together except Cheddar cheese; pour into a greased 13"x9" baking pan. Sprinkle with cheese; bake at 350 degrees for 30 to 40 minutes. Makes 12 servings.

Herb Garden Green Beans

Janet Pastrick
Gooseberry Patch

Fresh herbs really wake up the flavor of green beans
in this easy side dish.

1-1/2 c. water
1 lb. green beans, trimmed
4 T. butter
3 T. fresh chives, chopped

2 t. lemon zest
1/4 t. ground ginger
1/8 t. salt
1/4 t. pepper

Bring water to a full boil in a skillet; add beans. Heat over medium heat until tender, about 9 to 14 minutes; drain. Return to skillet; add remaining ingredients. Heat until thoroughly warmed, about 2 to 4 minutes, stirring occasionally. Makes 6 servings.

**Everybody wants to save the earth...nobody
wants to help Mom to do the dishes.
- P.J. O'Rourke**

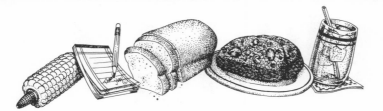

Green Bean & Corn Casserole

Cheryl Rucker
Flatwoods, KY

A perfect potluck dish...it's simple and tasty!

14-1/2 oz. can French-style
  green beans, drained
15-oz. can shoe peg corn,
  drained
1/2 c. Cheddar cheese, grated
1/2 c. sour cream
1/2 c. onion, chopped

10-3/4 oz. can cream of celery
  soup
1/8 t. salt
1/2 c. butter, melted
1 sleeve buttery round crackers,
  crushed
1/2 c. slivered almonds

Toss beans and corn together; spread in an ungreased 2-quart casserole dish. Mix cheese, sour cream, onion, soup, and salt together; pour over beans and corn. Mix butter and cracker crumbs together in another mixing bowl; spread over cheese mixture. Top with almonds; bake at 350 degrees for 45 minutes. Serves 8.

Travel tip: See how many things you can spot to eat
while you're traveling down the highway.
Choose things like chicken or vegetables
as well as words and pictures from passing signs.

BEEFY STU'S

Beef Burgundy

Melia Himich
Manchester, MI

*An easy-to-prepare dish that's delicious
served over noodles or rice.*

1-1/2 lb. sirloin beef, cubed
2 1-1/2 oz. pkgs. dry onion
    soup mix
2 10-3/4 oz. cans cream of
    mushroom soup

1/2 c. burgundy wine
1/2 c. water

Combine ingredients in a Dutch oven; bake at 325 degrees for
2-1/2 hours. Makes 6 to 8 servings.

Garden's Bounty Salad

Kristy Gamet
Matthews, NC

*The dressing is so delicious and complements
the natural flavor of the veggies.*

3/4 c. vinegar
1-1/2 t. celery salt
4-1/2 t. sugar
1/8 t. mustard seed
1/2 t. salt
2 drops hot pepper sauce

1/8 t. pepper
1/4 c. water
6 tomatoes, cut into wedges
1 sweet onion, sliced
1 cucumber, sliced
1 green pepper, sliced

Combine first 8 ingredients in a saucepan; bring to a boil for
one minute. Toss remaining ingredients together; pour hot dressing
over vegetables. Gently toss again; refrigerate several hours before
serving. Makes 6 servings.

**Put another dime in the jukebox and dance
with the one you love!**

Baked Corn

Melissa Garland
Annville, PA

We always make this for special occasions...it's a great side dish
for turkey, chicken or ham.

2 eggs, beaten
1 c. sour cream
15-oz. can creamed corn

15-1/4 oz. can corn
7-oz. pkg. corn muffin mix
1/2 c. butter, melted

Combine eggs and sour cream together; add creamed corn and corn, mixing well. Stir in muffin mix; add butter. Bake at 350 degrees in a lightly greased 8"x8" baking dish for 35 to 45 minutes. Makes 12 servings.

May you look back on the past with as much pleasure as you
look forward to the future.
– Paul Dickson

BEEFY STU'S

Beefy Stew

Donna Scheuerman
Warwick, NY

A hearty meal that satisfies everyone...serve with crusty bread!

1 c. all-purpose flour
salt and pepper to taste
1/8 t. onion powder
2 lbs. beef stew meat
2 T. oil
2 1-lb. cans peeled tomatoes

4 c. water
6 carrots, thickly sliced
4 onions, quartered
3 lbs. potatoes, peeled and quartered

Combine flour, salt, pepper and onion powder together; coat meat with flour mixture. Heat oil in large Dutch oven; brown meat and set aside. Blend tomatoes with water; pour into drippings in Dutch oven. Add meat and carrots; bring to a boil. Reduce heat and simmer 15 minutes; add onions and potatoes. Simmer 2-1/2 hours. Makes 8 servings.

Make homestyle stew just like the ones at your favorite diner...thicken soups and stews without using flour or cornstarch! Purée a few cooked veggies from the pot and stir them back into the stew for a hearty bowl everyone will enjoy.

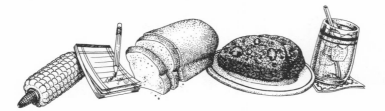

Garlic Mashed Potatoes

Karen Brockbank
Signal Hill, CA

These skin-on potatoes are so smooth & creamy!

4 redskin potatoes, cubed
4 T. butter

5-oz. can evaporated milk
1 clove garlic, minced

Boil potatoes in salted water until tender; mash. Add butter and milk; blend to desired consistency. Mix in garlic. Serves 2.

If your favorite casserole tends to drip in the oven, place a sheet of foil under the pan to catch drippings...clean up's a snap!

BEEFY STU'S

Poor Man's Steak

Elizabeth Andrus
Gooseberry Patch

Homemakers in the 1940's were delighted with the variety of foods they could prepare using canned soups. Inexpensive meats could be turned into flavorful dishes worthy enough to serve company!

2 lbs. ground beef
1/2 sleeve saltine crackers,
  crushed
1 egg, beaten
1 c. all-purpose flour
1/2 t. salt
1/2 t. pepper

1/2 c. margarine
10-3/4 oz. can cream of mushroom soup
10-3/4 oz. can chicken soup
1 c. hot water
1/8 t. Worcestershire sauce
2 t. beef bouillon granules

Combine beef, cracker crumbs and egg in a large mixing bowl. Form into one-inch thick patties; set aside. On a dinner plate, mix together flour, salt and pepper; coat patties. Brown both sides on medium heat, about 15 minutes per side. While cooking, whisk remaining ingredients together until smooth; pour into a 13"x9" baking pan. Arrange patties on top of soup mixture; bake at 350 degrees for 2-1/2 hours. Serves 8.

To keep the kids busy while traveling, draw road signs on a sheet of paper...when your child sees each sign, he or she can cross it off. Give a prize once all are crossed off.

Spaghetti & Meatballs

Sue Watt
Scotland, AR

This scrumptious recipe will have them asking for seconds!

46-oz. can tomato juice
2 6-oz. cans tomato paste
2 T. onion, chopped
4 t. sugar
1 t. salt
1 T. margarine
1 clove garlic, minced

1/2 c. water
2 bay leaves
2 t. celery salt
1 t. dried oregano
1 t. dried basil
16-oz. pkg. spaghetti, cooked
   and drained

Combine all ingredients except spaghetti; mix well. Simmer on low heat, stirring occasionally for 1-1/2 hours. Add meatballs to sauce; pour over spaghetti to serve. Serves 6.

Meatballs:

1 lb. ground beef
1/3 c. fresh parsley, chopped
1/2 c. bread crumbs
6 T. fresh Parmesan cheese,
   grated

1 egg
3 T. milk
2 t. salt
1 t. pepper
3 T. oil

Mix all ingredients except oil together; form into walnut-size balls. Brown in oil over medium heat, turning frequently until no longer pink inside. Add to sauce.

One cannot think well, love well, sleep well,

if one has not dined well.

– Virginia Woolf

BEEFY STU'S

Farmhouse Bread

Paula Kvarfordt
Idaho Falls, ID

This is my favorite bread recipe...it is moist and rises very evenly.

2 T. active dry yeast
1 c. warm water
4 c. warm milk
1/2 c. oil
6 T. sugar

2 T. salt
2-1/2 c. whole-wheat flour
8-1/2 c. all-purpose flour,
    divided

Sprinkle yeast into water; set aside. In a large mixing bowl, combine milk, oil, sugar and salt; add wheat flour and 2-1/2 cups all-purpose flour. Mix in yeast mixture; add remaining flour. Let rest for 10 minutes; knead for 5 minutes. Allow dough to double in bulk; punch down and allow to double in bulk again. Divide dough into quarters; place into four greased 9"x5" loaf pans and let double once more. Bake at 400 degrees for 5 minutes; reduce heat to 375 degrees and bake for 5 minutes; reduce heat to 350 degrees and bake for 20 minutes; reduce heat to 325 and bake for 5 minutes. Makes 4 loaves.

Make a trip to Sleeping Bear Dune National Seashore in Michigan...there are breathtaking views of awe-inspiring sand mountains, an incredible beach and Lake Michigan at your feet.

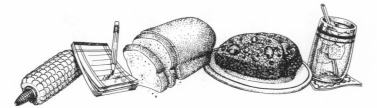

Harvest Veggie Soup

Anne Barrett
Pelham, NH

It's equally delicious served hot or cold.

2 T. olive oil
2 onions, chopped
5 c. chicken broth
2 potatoes, peeled and sliced
3 carrots, chopped

1 lb. zucchini, chopped
1 lb. summer squash, chopped
1 T. salt
1 t. pepper
4 T. fresh basil, chopped

Sauté onion in olive oil in a 4-quart stockpot over medium heat until tender; add broth and potatoes. Bring to a boil; cover and simmer for 5 minutes. Add carrots; simmer for 8 more minutes. Add zucchini, squash, salt and pepper; simmer another 15 minutes. Remove from heat; allow to cool. Add basil; process in small batches in a blender until smooth. Reheat before serving, if desired. Serves 6.

**Try serving munchies and finger foods from muffin tins.
It'll be a treat not soon forgotten.**

BEEFY STU'S

Cheddar-Chive Muffins

Casii Dodd
Frederick, MD

Warm, cheesy muffins are the perfect addition to any meal.

1/2 c. cornmeal
1 c. all-purpose flour
1 T. baking powder
1 T. sugar
1/2 t. salt
3/4 c. milk

1 egg, beaten
1 T. butter, melted
1 T. fresh chives, chopped
1/2 c. shredded sharp Cheddar
   cheese

Mix cornmeal, flour, baking powder, sugar and salt in a mixing bowl; slowly add milk, stirring until just mixed. Stir in egg, butter, chives and cheese; pour into greased muffin pans. Bake at 375 degrees for 25 minutes or until tester inserted in muffin center comes out clean. Makes 12 servings.

You feel good just stepping in the door of a diner. No one can resist the aroma of freshly brewed coffee or the sight of a sweet and juicy pie under glass!

Dip That's a Hit

Teresa Beal
Gooseberry Patch

*It's so simple and a sure-fire crowd-pleaser when served
with veggies, chips and pretzels.*

1/2 c. mayonnaise
1/4 c. sugar
2 T. horseradish mustard

1 t. oil
1 t. garlic powder

Combine ingredients together; cover and refrigerate 2 to 3 hours before serving. Makes about one cup.

Chilly Chocolate Malts

Connie Bryant
Topeka, KS

Best when sipped with two straws!

1 c. milk
1/2 c. caramel ice cream topping
2 c. chocolate ice cream,
    softened

3-1/2 T. malted milk powder
2 T. chopped pecans
Garnish: chocolate, grated

Combine first 5 ingredients in a blender; cover and blend until smooth. Pour into chilled glasses; sprinkle with grated chocolate. Makes 2-1/2 cups.

My mother's menu consisted of two choices: take it or leave it.
- Buddy Hackett

BEEFY STU'S

Green Chilie-Chicken Sandwiches

Donna Nowicki
Center City, NM

This spicy chicken is a quick & easy alternative to hamburgers.

4 boneless skinless chicken
   breast halves
2/3 c. soy sauce
1/4 c. cider vinegar
2 T. sugar
2 t. oil

4-oz. can whole green chilies,
   drained and sliced
   lengthwise
4 slices Pepper Jack cheese
4 kaiser rolls, split

Flatten chicken; place in resealable plastic bag. Combine soy sauce, vinegar, sugar and oil in a mixing bowl; set aside 1/4 cup. Pour remaining marinade over chicken; seal bag and turn to coat. Refrigerate for 30 minutes; drain and discard marinade. Grill chicken, uncovered, over medium heat for 3 minutes. Turn and baste with reserved marinade; grill 3 minutes longer or until juices run clear when pierced with a fork. Top each breast with one green chilie and cheese slice; cover and grill for 2 more minutes or until cheese is melted. Serve on rolls. Makes 4 servings.

A collection of retro tins is a great way to remember the past...group fun colors, patterns and shapes together.

Zesty Minestrone

Beth Hagopian
Huntsville, AL

This soup reheats well and is the perfect addition to any lunch box.

1 lb. Italian sausage, sliced
2 t. oil
1 onion, chopped
1 green pepper, chopped
3 cloves garlic, chopped
2 16-oz. cans whole tomatoes
2 potatoes, chopped
1/4 c. fresh parsley, chopped

2 t. dried oregano
1 t. dried basil
1 t. fennel seed
1/2 t. red pepper flakes
salt and pepper to taste
1 qt. beef broth
2 16-oz. cans kidney beans
1 c. elbow macaroni, uncooked

Sauté sausage in oil in a large saucepan; drain. Add onion, green pepper and garlic; cook 5 minutes. Pour in tomatoes, potatoes, spices and broth; bring to a boil. Reduce heat; simmer 30 minutes. Stir in beans and pasta; simmer an additional 20 minutes. Makes 6 to 8 servings.

Baking soda can bring out the natural sweetness of tomato sauce by reducing the acid. Add about 1/4 teaspoon per quart of sauce as it simmers.

BEEFY STU'S

Quick & Easy Shepherd's Pie

Toni Wilcox
Winter Park, FL

This low-fuss meal makes delicious leftovers...if you have any!

1-1/4 lb. ground beef
1 onion, chopped
8-oz. can tomato sauce
8-oz. can green beans, drained
8-oz. can corn, drained
1/4 t. cumin
1/2 t. garlic powder

1/4 t. salt
1-lb. pkg. refrigerated mashed
   potatoes
1 egg, beaten
2-1/2 c. shredded Monterey Jack
   cheese, divided

Brown ground beef with onion; drain. Stir in tomato sauce, green beans, corn, cumin, garlic powder and salt; simmer while preparing mashed potatoes according to package directions. In a separate mixing bowl, combine egg and 2 cups cheese; spread in the bottom of a lightly greased 8"x8" baking pan. Spoon meat mixture over the cheese; spread potatoes on top. Sprinkle with remaining cheese; bake at 375 degrees for 20 to 30 minutes. Let stand 5 minutes before serving. Makes 9 servings.

Keep your dinner piping hot to enjoy at picnics, family
reunions or a day out on the lake. Just line a cooler with foil
and take it along anywhere...a hot meal on-the-go!

Creamy Classic Macaroni & Cheese

Shelli Wells
Dublin, OH

*Serve it as a main dish or a side...either way, this dish
will get rave reviews.*

2 T. butter, melted
2 T. all-purpose flour
1 c. milk
1/2 t. salt
1 t. dry mustard

1/4 c. shredded mozzarella
  cheese
8-oz. box elbow macaroni,
  uncooked
4 slices American cheese

Whisk butter and flour together until smooth; place in saucepan over
medium heat. Add milk, salt and mustard; stir until thickened.
Gradually add mozzarella cheese; stir until melted. Remove from heat.
Cook elbow macaroni for half the cooking time listed on the box; drain
and set aside. Lightly grease an 8"x8" baking dish, pour in cheese
mixture and pasta; stir well. Top with slices of American cheese; bake
in a 350 degree oven for 30 to 40 minutes or until lightly brown and
bubbly. Serves 4.

**When preparing to travel, lay out all your clothes and all your
money. Then take half the clothes and twice the money.**
– Susan Heller

BEEFY STU'S

Peanut Butter Cup Cookies

Gini Green
Lakewood, CA

These are my husband's all-time favorite cookies!

1 c. shortening
1 c. sugar
1 c. brown sugar, packed
1 t. vanilla extract
2 eggs, beaten

1 c. creamy peanut butter
3 c. all-purpose flour
2 t. baking soda
1/8 t. salt
72 small peanut butter cups

Cream shortening, sugars and vanilla; add eggs and beat thoroughly. Stir in peanut butter; set aside. Sift dry ingredients together; blend into creamed mixture. Form dough into one-inch balls; place into greased mini muffin tins. Bake at 375 degrees for 10 to 12 minutes; remove from oven. Press one peanut butter cup into the center of each cookie; cool 10 minutes then carefully remove from tins. Makes about 6 dozen.

Everyone in the car can have fun with traveling tongue twisters: Please pass the plate of pickles to Polly. Silly Sammy sells souvenir spoons. Susie went to Sioux City to see her sister Sally.

Italian Pie

Becky Hawkins
Spearfish, SD

Serve with a Caesar salad for a complete meal.

1 lb. ground beef, browned
garlic salt and pepper to taste
16-oz. jar spaghetti sauce
2 8-oz. cans refrigerated cres-
    cent rolls

1/2 c. shredded mozzarella
    cheese
1/2 c. shredded Colby cheese

Season browned beef with garlic salt and pepper to taste; add spaghetti sauce and simmer for 5 minutes. Layer one can of crescent rolls on the bottom of a greased 13"x9" baking dish; spread rolls to edges of pan. Pour spaghetti sauce over rolls; layer cheeses on top. Spread remaining can of crescent rolls over the cheese layer; cover with aluminum foil. Bake at 350 degrees for 30 minutes, remove cover and bake 15 more minutes. Makes 12 servings.

Give the world the best that you have,
and the best will come back to you.
– Madeline Bridges

BEEFY STU'S

Stuffed Manicotti

DeNeane Deskins
Marengo, OH

*This hearty manicotti with homemade sauce is sure
to become a family favorite.*

1/4 lb. sausage
1/2 lb. ground beef
2 T. olive oil
2 T. onion, chopped
2 T. green pepper, chopped
homemade sauce

1/4 c. bread crumbs
1/2 T. fresh parsley, chopped
salt and pepper to taste
8-oz. pkg. manicotti shells,
   uncooked
1/2 c. mozzarella cheese, grated

Brown sausage and ground beef in oil with onion and green pepper; drain and set aside. When cooled, combine with 2 tablespoons sauce, bread crumbs, parsley, salt and pepper; fill manicotti with mixture. Pour 1/4 cup sauce in bottom of a 13"x9" baking dish; arrange filled manicotti on top. Cover with remaining sauce; sprinkle with cheese. Bake at 400 degrees for 40 minutes. Makes 8 servings.

Homemade Sauce:

6 T. olive oil
1 clove garlic, minced
1 onion, minced
2 T. fresh parsley, chopped
2 32-oz. cans whole tomatoes

16-oz. can tomato sauce
salt and pepper to taste
1 t. sugar
1 t. dried basil

Heat olive oil in sauce pan; add garlic, onion and parsley. Pour in tomatoes, tomato sauce and seasonings; simmer, uncovered, until thickened, about 20 minutes.

**Let your family know what's in store for them
at dinnertime...hang up a vintage chalkboard
to announce today's specials!**

Cream of Broccoli Soup

Julie Woodring
Osceola Mills, PA

Also delicious when prepared with cauliflower.

1 c. water
2 bunches broccoli, chopped
2 c. milk
2 c. white Cheddar cheese, cubed

1/2 c. all-purpose flour
1 c. half-and-half
2 cubes chicken bouillon
Garnish: croutons

Cook broccoli in water until tender; do not drain. Place milk, cheese and flour in a blender; process until mixed. Combine blended mix, broccoli mix, half-and-half and chicken bouillon cubes; cook over medium heat until thickened, stirring gently. Pour into bowls; garnish with croutons. Makes 6 to 8 servings.

In America there are two classes of travel...
first class and with children.
– Horace Benchly

BEEFY
STU'S

Chicken Pot Pie

Gail Goudy
Walls, MS

Our family loves to have this meal on a cold night.

5 boneless skinless chicken
breasts, boiled and cubed
10-3/4 oz. can cream of chicken
soup
10-3/4 oz. can cream of celery
soup

15-oz. can mixed vegetables
1/2 c. onion, chopped
2 c. chicken broth

Place chicken in a 13"x9" baking dish; set aside. Combine remaining
ingredients; pour over chicken. Top with crust batter; bake at
400 degrees for 45 minutes or until golden brown. Makes 12 servings.

Crust:

1 c. self-rising flour
1 t. baking powder

1/2 c. margarine, melted
1 c. milk

Combine ingredients; mix well. Spread evenly over chicken mixture.

**Take a trip down memory lane...remember pulling out an LP or
45-rpm from the original jacket?**

Ambrosia

Jennifer Price
Philadelphia, PA

The tropical flavors of orange, pineapple and coconut blend
to make this a refreshing dessert.

11-oz. can mandarin oranges,
   drained
10-1/2 oz. bag mini marshmallows, divided
8-oz. carton whipped topping
2/3 c. flaked coconut

6-oz. jar maraschino cherries,
   drained
1 c. sour cream
8-oz. can crushed pineapple,
   drained

Gently combine oranges, whipped topping, cherries, sour cream, pineapple, coconut and one-half bag mini marshmallows, saving the remainder for another recipe. Refrigerate well-blended mixture before serving. Makes 6 servings.

A tipped waitress doesn't spill.
– 1950's Diner Sign

CHOCOLATE CREAM PIE
15¢ slice

BEEFY STU'S

Amish Sugar Cookies

Melissa Phillips
Meadville, PA

Keep a batch of these cookies in the freezer...when guests are dropping by, simply thaw and enjoy.

3 c. sugar, divided
1-1/2 c. shortening
2 eggs
1-1/2 c. milk
6 c. all-purpose flour

3 t. baking powder
1-1/2 t. baking soda
1/2 T. vanilla extract
1/2 t. salt

Mix all ingredients together reserving one cup sugar; refrigerate 2 hours. Roll dough out on a lightly floured surface to 1/4-inch thickness; use cookie cutters to cut into desired shapes. Sprinkle with remaining sugar; bake at 350 degrees on a lightly greased baking sheet for 10 minutes. Makes 6 to 7 dozen.

Prepare a diner delight by scooping orange or lime sherbet and vanilla ice cream in chilled parfait glasses or sherbet cups.

Oma's Streusel Cake

Cindy Kolpek
Glendale, AZ

For an added bonus, layer sliced apples over cake
before adding streusel!

3/4 c. butter
1 c. sugar
2 eggs

3-1/2 c. all-purpose flour
4 t. baking powder
1-1/4 c. milk

Cream butter, sugar and eggs together; slowly add flour, baking powder and milk, alternately. Add additional milk if dough is too stiff; spread into a lightly greased and floured 13"x9" baking pan. Sprinkle with streusel; bake at 350 degrees for 45 minutes. Makes 12 to 15 servings.

Streusel:

3/4 c. butter
1 c. sugar

1 t. vanilla extract
2-3/4 c. all-purpose flour

Mix ingredients by hand until dry and crumbly.

BEEFY STU'S

Cherry-Filled Oatmeal Cookies

Jennifer Strehlow
Liberty, MO

My grandma taught me how to make these cookies...I like to nibble around the edges to savor the sweet, gooey filling.

2 eggs, beaten
1 c. brown sugar, packed
1 c. sugar
3/4 c. oil
1 t. vanilla extract
1/4 t. salt
1 t. baking soda

1 t. baking powder
2 c. all-purpose flour
2 c. quick-cooking oats,
   uncooked
1 c. flaked coconut
14-1/2 oz. can cherry pie filling

Beat eggs and sugars together; add oil, vanilla and dry ingredients. Knead dough slightly; roll into an equal amount of one-inch balls and dime-sized balls. Place one-inch balls on a baking sheet; slightly flatten with a fork dipped in cold water. Place one cherry along with a small amount of pie filling on top of each cookie; flatten dime-sized balls and cover filling and cherry. Bake at 350 degrees for 10 minutes or until light golden brown. Makes 3 dozen.

Buy postcards of the places you go and, on the back of each one, have your kids write down what they want to remember. At the end of the trip, punch a hole in the corner of each postcard and place them on a ring as a special memento.

Black Raspberry Pie

Roberta Scheeler
Gooseberry Patch

*Nothing goes better with a steaming cup of java than
a thick slice of black raspberry pie.*

1 qt. black raspberries
2 9-inch pie crusts, unbaked

1 c. plus 1 T. sugar, divided
3-1/2 T. all-purpose flour

Place raspberries into bottom pie crust; set aside. Combine one cup sugar and flour; pour over berries. Place top crust on pie and flute edges. Sprinkle remaining sugar on top; vent top crust. Bake at 350 degrees for one hour. Makes 8 servings.

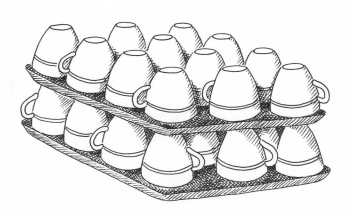

Capture a vacation memory forever...collect souvenir
matchbooks from favorite restaurants or shops and
show them off in a vintage glass jar.

BEEFY
STU'S

Blueberries & Cream Pull-Aparts

Margaret Scoresby
Mount Vernon, OH

This recipe makes 2 pans...one to eat and one to share!

2 c. milk, scalded
1 T. active dry yeast
1/3 c. oil
1 t. salt
1/3 c. sugar
5 to 6 c. all-purpose flour

2 eggs, beaten
1 c. butter, melted and divided
3-1/2 oz. box instant vanilla
    pudding mix
1 c. blueberries

Let yeast sit in cooled scalded milk for 10 minutes; mix with oil, salt, sugar, flour and eggs. Allow dough to double in bulk; roll out on a lightly floured surface to 1/2-inch thickness. Cut dough with a biscuit cutter or round glass into about 30 rounds. Pour 1/2 cup butter into each of two Bundt® pans; dip rounds in butter then in vanilla pudding mix. Line sides and bottom of pans with rounds, overlapping edges, using 15 per pan. Sprinkle blueberries between rounds; bake at 400 degrees for 20 minutes. Makes about 15 servings per pan.

Other things may change us,
but we start and end with family.
– Anthony Brandt

Rhubarb Cake

Beth Anstedt
Sparta, NJ

This sweet, moist cake is the perfect way to top off a good meal!

1/2 c. shortening
1-1/2 c. brown sugar, packed
1 egg
2 c. all-purpose flour
1/2 t. baking soda

1/2 t. salt
1 c. buttermilk
1-1/2 c. rhubarb, thickly sliced
Garnish: whipped topping

Combine shortening, sugar and egg; beat until light and fluffy. In a separate mixing bowl, mix flour, soda and salt together; add to shortening mixture alternately with buttermilk. Fold in rhubarb; mix well. Pour into a greased and floured 13"x9" baking pan; bake at 350 degrees for 30 to 40 minutes. Top with whipped topping before serving. Makes 12 to 15 servings.

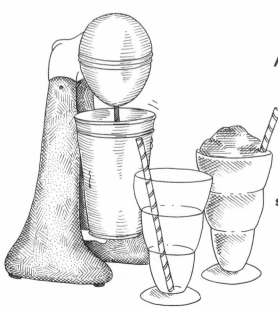

America has a love affair with the diner...people know that the sight of a diner means real home-cooked meals served at reasonable prices in a clean, comfortable atmosphere.

BEEFY STU'S

Decadent Pumpkin Bread

Bonnie Quigley
New Canaan, CT

Bake in 2 large loaf pans or separate into seven mini loaf pans for individual treats.

1/2 c. butter, softened
2-2/3 c. sugar
4 eggs
16-oz. can pumpkin
2/3 c. water
3-1/3 c. all-purpose flour
2 t. baking soda

1-1/2 t. salt
1-1/2 t. baking powder
1 t. cinnamon
1 t. ground cloves
2/3 c. chopped walnuts
1-1/4 c. chocolate chips

Cream butter and sugar together; beat in eggs, pumpkin and water. Blend in dry ingredients; fold in nuts and chocolate chips. Divide and pour into 2 greased 9"x5" loaf pans; bake at 350 degrees for 65 minutes. Serves 8 to 10 per loaf.

Avoid the turnpike by taking a "shunpike" trip. Taking the back roads allows even the driver to enjoy the scenery.

Oatmeal-Coconut Fudgies

Dora Dayton
Lakewood, OH

These portable cookies are perfect for picnics.

1/2 c. butter
1/2 c. milk
2 c. sugar
1/2 c. baking cocoa

2 c. quick-cooking oats,
  uncooked
1/2 c. flaked coconut

Bring butter, milk, sugar and cocoa to a boil, stirring often; boil 5 minutes. Remove from heat; stir in remaining ingredients. Drop by tablespoonfuls onto wax paper. Makes about 4 dozen.

Lemon-Cherry Sipper

Kathy Lowe
Orem, UT

It's like drinking liquid sunshine!

1-3/4 c. fresh-squeezed lemon
  juice
1 c. sugar

1 lb. fresh cherries, pitted
3 qts. water

Combine lemon juice and sugar in a one-gallon container; shake until sugar is dissolved. Add 3 quarts water and cherries; stir well. Fill glasses with ice and juice. Makes 6 to 8 servings.

BEEFY STU'S

Strawberry Bread

Laura Kennemuth
Anderson, IN

Once you make this yummy dessert for guests,
they'll request it again & again!

1-1/2 c. sugar
1-1/4 c. oil
4 eggs
3 c. all-purpose flour
1 t. baking soda

1 t. cinnamon
1 t. salt
2 10-oz. pkgs. frozen strawberries, thawed and divided

Blend sugar and oil together; add eggs, one at a time, mixing thoroughly after each addition. Combine dry ingredients in a separate mixing bowl; set aside. Reserve 1/2 cup strawberries for sauce. Add half the dry ingredients and half the remaining strawberries to the egg mixture; mix on low until combined. Mix in remaining halves well; divide dough and pour in 2 greased and floured 8"x4" loaf pans. Bake at 350 degrees for 50 minutes. Cool; slice and serve with strawberry sauce. Makes 8 servings per loaf.

Sauce:

8-oz. pkg. cream cheese,
 softened
2 T. sugar

1/2 c. reserved strawberries,
 puréed

Combine ingredients until spreading consistency is achieved.

**Capture the flavor of the diner! Fill a jar with penny
candy and licorice snaps. Just like the one next
to the register!**

White Chocolate-Orange Dreams

Jessica Parker
Mulvane, KS

Creamy white chocolate and sweet orange make these cookies a refreshing snack anytime.

1 c. butter, softened
2/3 c. brown sugar, packed
1/2 c. sugar
1 egg
1 T. orange zest
2 t. orange extract

2-1/4 c. all-purpose flour
3/4 t. baking soda
1/2 t. salt
12-oz. pkg. white chocolate
  chips

Cream butter and sugars together until creamy; add egg, orange zest and orange extract, blending well. In a separate mixing bowl, combine flour, baking soda and salt; gradually add to sugar mixture, blending after each addition. Fold in chocolate chips; drop dough by rounded tablespoonfuls onto ungreased baking sheets. Bake at 350 degrees for 10 to 12 minutes or until edges are lightly brown. Cool for 2 minutes before removing from baking sheet. Makes about 3-1/2 dozen.

Sodas just seem to taste better in old-fashioned parfait glasses! Add ice cream, your favorite toppings and a striped straw...guaranteed smiles!

Whistlin' Dixie

diner

Southern fare that'll stick to your ribs.

Grits Au Gratin

Debi Gilpin
Bluefield, WV

Quick and versatile, this side is great for breakfast, lunch or dinner.

3 c. water
3/4 c. quick-cooking grits
1 t. salt
1/4 lb. sharp Cheddar cheese,
   thinly sliced

1/2 c. milk
1/2 c. bread crumbs
1 T. butter, melted
1/4 t. paprika

Bring water to a boil; stir in grits and salt. Heat for 2-1/2 to 5 minutes; remove from heat. Alternate layers of grits and cheese in a 1-1/2 quart casserole dish; pour milk over the top. In a separate bowl, toss bread crumbs and butter together; sprinkle over casserole. Sprinkle with paprika; bake at 325 degrees for about 20 to 25 minutes. Makes 4 servings.

Hearty Creamed Eggs & Toast

Ruby McFarland
Monticello, KY

A perfect start to any day...so warm & rich!

2 10-3/4 oz. cans cream of
   mushroom soup
milk

6 eggs, hard-boiled, peeled and
   sliced
8 to 10 slices bread, toasted

Heat soup and one soup can of milk in a large saucepan; add eggs. Continue cooking, stirring frequently, until mixture is warmed but not boiling. Serve over toast. Makes 8 to 10 servings.

Snacks to go! Line a vintage wire basket with a pretty
checked towel and fill it with pretzels, popcorn
or snack mix...yummy!

Whistlin' Dixie
diner

Baked Oatmeal

Vanessa Longenecker
Lancaster, PA

*This is my 4 year-old's favorite breakfast. You can
even save time and make it the night before!*

3 c. long-cooking oats,
   uncooked
3/4 c. brown sugar, packed
1/2 c. butter
2 eggs

2 c. milk
2 t. baking powder
1 t. salt
1/2 t. cinnamon
1 t. vanilla extract

Combine ingredients together; mix well. Pour into a buttered 2-quart
casserole dish; bake at 375 degrees for 25 minutes. Makes
6 servings.

BREAKFAST
★ served ★
ALL DAY

**Serve up diner-style oatmeal...brown sugar, honey and fruit
preserves are a great way to add new flavors
to an old favorite!**

Farmhouse Breakfast

Kathy Grashoff
Fort Wayne, IN

Serve hot with warm maple syrup.

8 sausage links, sliced
6 tart apples, sliced
3/4 c. brown sugar, packed

1 c. apple cider
12-oz. can refrigerated
  buttermilk biscuits

Arrange sausage slices in a 8"x8" baking pan; layer apples, brown sugar and cider on top. Bake at 400 degrees for 15 minutes; layer biscuits over sausages and apples. Baste with juices; lower oven temperature to 350 degrees and bake an additional 30 minutes. Serves 4 to 6.

For a fresh-picked centerpiece, pile green apples on a breadboard and tuck in white daisies among the apples...delightful!

Whistlin' Dixie
diner

Sizzlin' Ham Patties

Pat Canterbury
Harmony, MN

This is a favorite of my children and grandchildren!

1 ham bone
6 c. water
1 c. cornmeal
1-1/2 c. cooked ham, diced

1/2 t. dried sage
1 c. all-purpose flour
1/3 c. shortening

Boil ham bone in water; strain, reserving 4 cups ham broth. Bring ham broth to a boil in a saucepan; add cornmeal. Cook 10 minutes; stirring often. Add ham and sage; heat for 15 more minutes. Pour into a greased 9"x5" loaf pan; chill until set. Slice into 1/2-inch thick slices; coat with flour and set aside. Melt shortening in a skillet; brown ham on both sides. Makes 8 to 10 servings.

Apple Fritter Rings

Carol Hickman
Kingsport, TN

Try serving with a big scoop of vanilla ice cream and a drizzle of honey.

1 egg, beaten
2/3 c. milk
1 t. oil
1 c. all-purpose flour
1/4 c. plus 2 T. sugar, divided
1 t. baking powder

1/8 t. salt
5 Granny Smith apples, peeled, cored and thickly sliced
1/2 t. cinnamon
oil for deep-frying

Combine egg, milk and oil; set aside. Mix flour, 2 tablespoons sugar, baking powder and salt together; blend into egg mixture until smooth. Dip apple rings into batter; deep-fry in 365 degree oil until golden brown on both sides. Drain; sprinkle with mixture of remaining sugar and cinnamon. Makes 2 dozen.

Finger Lickin' Chicken Wings

Berniece Boyett
Rogers, AR

Great to make ahead...just pop in the microwave to reheat!

4-oz. bottle soy sauce
1/3 c. brown sugar, packed
1 t. fresh ginger root, grated

2 cloves garlic, minced
1 t. Dijon mustard
2 doz. chicken wings

Blend all ingredients except chicken wings together; marinate wings in mixture overnight. Bake wings in a 350-degree oven for one hour; baste after 30 minutes with marinade; discard remaining marinade. Makes 4 servings.

For a refreshing twist on an old-fashioned favorite, float a thinly sliced orange in a pitcher of fresh-squeezed lemonade...delicious!

Whistlin' Dixie
diner

Barbecue Cups

Lori VanRyckeghem
Bellevue, NE

Finger foods you can take along anywhere.

3/4 lb. ground beef, browned
   and drained
1/2 c. barbecue sauce
1 T. dry minced onion

2 T. brown sugar, packed
12-oz. can refrigerated biscuits
3/4 c. shredded Cheddar cheese

Add sauce, onion and brown sugar to ground beef; mix well and set aside. Separate biscuits; place in ungreased muffin tins. Press dough along sides of muffin tins; divide meat mixture between muffins. Sprinkle with cheese; bake at 400 degrees for 10 to 12 minutes. Makes 10 servings.

Miss Aimee B.'s Lemonade

Judy Kelly
St. Louis, MO

The addition of milk adds a new twist to an age-old classic.

2 lemons
1-1/2 c. sugar
2 c. milk

3 c. club soda, divided
3 c. crushed ice, divided

Slice off ends and then quarter lemons; squeeze juice into a bowl and set aside. Coarsely chop lemon quarters in a blender; add to juice. Stir in sugar; set aside for 30 minutes. Add milk; stir well. Cover and refrigerate overnight. Strain mixture; discard solids. To serve, fill a glass with 1/2 cup lemonade mixture, 1/2 cup club soda and 1/2 cup crushed ice; stir well. Makes 6 servings.

Baked Sweet Onion Spread

Linda Hendrix
Moundville, MO

Double, triple, quadruple...and serve with crackers and bread sticks!

1 c. sweet onion, finely chopped
1/2 c. mayonnaise
1/2 c. sharp Cheddar cheese,
   grated
1/4 t. hot pepper sauce
1/4 c. fresh Parmesan cheese,
   grated
paprika to taste

Combine onion, mayonnaise, Cheddar cheese and hot pepper sauce together; spread into a 7"x7" oven-proof dish. Top with Parmesan cheese; sprinkle with paprika. Bake at 350 degrees for 25 to 30 minutes. Serves 6.

Black-Eyed Pea Dip

Susan Boss
Loganville, GA

Serve warm with tortilla chips.

3 16-oz. cans black-eyed peas,
   drained and rinsed
2 c. shredded sharp Cheddar
   cheese
4-oz. can chopped green chilies,
   drained
1/2 c. butter, melted
2 T. dry minced onion
1/4 t. garlic salt

Combine all ingredients in a large microwave-safe bowl; heat on medium-high power for 6 minutes, stirring every 2 minutes. Refrigerate in an airtight container. Makes 8 cups.

The secret to staying young is to live honestly, eat slowly and lie about your age.
– Lucille Ball

Whistlin' Dixie
diner

Deep-Fried Country Pickles

Dawn Smith
Cape Girardreau, MO

Use a mixture of different pickles for a southern surprise in every bite!

16-oz. jar sliced pickles
3 c. all-purpose flour
salt and pepper to taste

1 c. milk
oil for deep-frying
Garnish: catsup and salsa

Drain pickle slices on a paper towel. Toss flour, salt and pepper together in a medium mixing bowl; set aside. Dip pickle slices in milk; coat with flour mixture. Drop in 350-degree oil for 3 to 4 minutes or until crispy and golden brown. Drain; serve with catsup or salsa. Makes 5 servings.

Enjoy your retro tablecloths and vintage towels at your next picnic...they're a creative alternative to paper and plastic and lots more fun.

BBQ Beef Sandwiches

Karen Chandler
Madison Heights, MI

A little of this...a little of that, but lotsa taste guaranteed!

5 T. brown sugar, packed and
   divided
3/4 t. pepper
2 1-lb. flank steaks
1 c. onion, chopped
1 c. tomato paste
3 T. Worcestershire sauce
1 T. molasses

3 T. cider vinegar
1 T. chili powder
1 t. garlic powder
1 t. dry mustard
1 t. cumin
1/2 t. salt
10 submarine rolls

Combine one tablespoon brown sugar and pepper; rub onto both sides of steaks and set aside. Stir together the remaining ingredients except for the rolls in a slow cooker; add steaks, turning to coat. Cover and heat on high one hour; reduce heat to low and cook 7 hours. Remove steaks; reserve sauce. Shred steaks with 2 forks; return to cooker. Stir meat and sauce together; spoon onto rolls. Makes 10 servings.

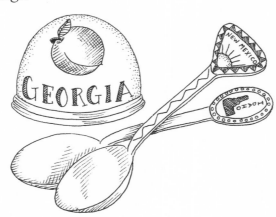

Dry your clothes on a clothesline in the sunshine...the fresh, clean smell will bring back memories and smiles.

Whistlin' Dixie
diner

Blue-Ribbon Barbeque Ribs

Denise Hooper
St. Cloud, MN

*Have plenty of napkins on hand when serving
these...messy but oh-so delicious.*

3/4 c. catsup
3/4 c. water
1 c. onion, chopped
2 T. sugar
1 T. Worcestershire sauce

1/4 t. paprika
1/4 t. red pepper
1/4 t. chili powder
2 lbs. pork spareribs

Combine all ingredients except the ribs in a saucepan; bring to a boil.
Place ribs in a greased 13"x9" baking pan; pour sauce over ribs. Bake
in a 375 degree oven for 1-1/2 hours. Serves 4.

Cornmeal-Fried Okra

Diane Gregory
Sheridan, AR

Try these dipped in ranch dressing for a homestyle snack.

1 lb. okra, trimmed and sliced
2 eggs, beaten
2/3 c. cornmeal

1 t. salt
1/2 t. pepper
oil for deep frying

Dip okra into beaten eggs; set aside. Combine cornmeal, salt and
pepper in a medium mixing bowl; add okra and toss to coat. Heat oil
in a large skillet over medium-high heat; fry okra until golden brown
on both sides, turning once. Drain on paper towels before serving.
Makes 4 servings.

**Go American! Choose one night a week to prepare dishes
specific to a region of our great country. Try barbecue for a
southern dinner or have a spicy southwestern fiesta!**

Garlic-Roasted Chicken & Potatoes

Cindy Corbett
West Caldwell, NJ

The secret's in the maple syrup glaze.

1/4 c. butter, melted
6 chicken drumsticks
6 potatoes, peeled and chopped
8 cloves garlic, unpeeled

2 t. salt, divided
1/8 t. pepper
1/4 c. maple syrup

Pour butter into a 17"x11" baking pan; place chicken, potatoes and garlic in pan. Sprinkle with one teaspoon salt and pepper; turn chicken to coat. Bake at 400 degrees 40 minutes, basting chicken and potatoes occasionally. Mix maple syrup with remaining salt; brush over chicken and potatoes. Bake 20 minutes longer; before serving. squeeze roasted garlic over chicken and potatoes. Makes 6 servings.

Old-fashioned diners received fruit & vegetable deliveries in wooden crates...pick up these crates at tag sales to hold kitchen towels, potholders and tablecloths in your kitchen!

Whistlin' Dixie
diner

Buttery Farm Biscuits

Kelly Hart
Pembroke, NH

*Try adding Parmesan cheese, basil and oregano or
grated orange peel, cinnamon and sugar!*

2 c. all-purpose flour
1 T. baking powder
1/4 t. salt

1/4 c. chilled butter, sliced
3/4 c. milk

Combine dry ingredients in a large mixing bowl; cut in butter until
mixture resembles coarse crumbs. Stir in milk with a fork until a soft
dough forms; roll into a large ball. Place dough on a lightly floured
baking sheet; press into a 6"x6" square. Cut dough into 12 square
biscuits but do not separate; bake at 400 degrees for 15 to 20 minutes
or until lightly golden brown. Makes 12.

Celebrate the happiness that friends are always giving,
make every day a holiday and just celebrate living.
– Amanda Bradley

Harlequin Chicken

Allene Ofcky
Manteno, IL

Real mayo is a must in this old-fashioned southern favorite.

3 to 5-lb. pkg. chicken pieces
3/4 c. mayonnaise
1 c. bread crumbs
1/2 t. onion salt

1/2 t. garlic salt
1/8 t. pepper
1/2 t. poultry seasoning

Rinse chicken; pat dry. Coat chicken with mayonnaise; set aside. Toss remaining ingredients together; sprinkle over chicken. Place chicken, breast side up, in a greased 13"x9" baking pan; bake at 375 degrees for 50 minutes or until juices from chicken run clear when pierced with a fork. Makes 4 to 6 servings.

Peachy Chicken Picante

Julie Sweet
Hartford, MI

Sweet & spicy...try it served over steamed rice.

1 lb. cooked chicken, cubed
1 T. taco seasoning
2 t. oil

1/3 c. peach preserves
8-oz. jar salsa

Coat chicken with taco seasoning; cook in oil over medium heat until juices run clear when pierced with a fork. Add preserves and salsa; simmer 15 to 20 minutes. Makes 4 servings.

Keep five or ten grains of rice inside your salt shaker to prevent it from clogging. A few peppercorns in your pepper shaker will do the same for your pepper and add a fresh taste too!

Whistlin' Dixie
diner

Cayenne Fried Chicken

Vickie

Warm up with this hot & spicy version of classic fried chicken...we guarantee you'll come back for seconds!

4 boneless skinless chicken
   breasts
2-1/2 c. milk
2 T. plus 4 drops hot pepper
   sauce
1 t. salt

3/4 c. all-purpose flour, divided
3/4 c. butter, melted
6 T. oil
1/2 t. garlic powder
1 t. fresh chives, chopped
salt and pepper to taste

Place chicken in a deep bowl, cover with milk; add 2 tablespoons hot pepper sauce and salt. Soak for one hour. Remove chicken and coat with 6 tablespoons flour; set milk mixture aside. Heat 1/3 cup butter and oil in a large skillet; brown chicken on both sides and set aside. Drain, reserving 3 tablespoons drippings in skillet; add remaining butter and flour, stirring until browned. Pour reserved milk into flour mixture; add garlic powder, chives, remaining hot pepper sauce, salt and pepper to taste. Heat thoroughly, stirring constantly. Pour over chicken before serving. Serves 4.

Save leftovers for a special night. Print out a menu to let everyone know what is available...let them choose their favorite!

Cajun Stuffed Roast

Misty Tauzin
Omaha, NE

*My mother-in-law from Lafayette, Louisiana traditionally serves this
sliced over rice for her whole family...it's truly delicious.*

3 to 5-lb. pot roast
5 cloves garlic, chopped
1 green pepper, chopped
1 onion, chopped

1 T. creole seasoning
1/8 t. pepper
3 T. oil
cold water

Cut criss-cross slices about 1/2-inch deep across top of roast; set
aside. Combine garlic, green pepper and onion together; spread into
slits on roast. Sprinkle with creole seasoning and pepper. Sear both
sides of roast in oil in a Dutch oven; add cold water to cover. Bring
to a boil; reduce heat and simmer for 3 to 4 hours or until tender.
Serves 6 to 8.

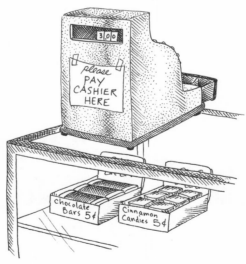

**Restaurantware is a whimsical way to set a diner-style
table...pick up pieces at flea markets & antique shops
decorated with everything from cowboys to railroads!**

Whistlin' Dixie
diner

Louisiana Swirl Muffins

Tami Bowman
Gooseberry Patch

*Perfect alongside any southern fare...just right
to nibble on for a snack too!*

2 c. all-purpose flour
1 T. baking powder
1 t. salt
1/2 c. butter, softened and
    divided
3/4 c. milk

1/2 c. grated Parmesan cheese
1/2 t. cayenne pepper
1 t. dried thyme
1/2 t. paprika
1 t. garlic salt

Mix flour, baking powder and salt; cut in 5 tablespoons butter until
coarse crumbs form. Stir in milk until dough forms a ball; knead on a
lightly floured surface. Roll to 1/2-inch thickness; spread with
remaining butter. Combine remaining ingredients in a small bowl;
sprinkle over buttered surface. Roll jelly roll-style; press seam to seal.
Place seam side down; cut into 12 slices. Push up underneath the
center of each slice to slightly raise center of swirl; place in greased
muffin pans. Bake at 425 degrees for 10 to 15 minutes or until
golden. Makes 12.

assorted
PASTRIES
10¢ *ea.*

**Good things baked in the kitchen will keep romance
far longer than bright lipstick.
-Marjorie Husted**

129

Cola Pork Chops

Maxine Chevrier
Twinsburg, OH

Melt-in-your-mouth tender and so easy.

8 pork chops
salt and pepper to taste
1 c. catsup

1 c. cola soda
4 T. brown sugar, packed

Place pork chops in a 13"x9" baking dish; season with salt and pepper. Mix catsup and cola together; pour over pork chops. Sprinkle with brown sugar; bake, uncovered, at 350 degrees for one hour or until tender. Serves 8.

Cheesy Potatoes

Becky Martin
Machesney Park, IL

Creamy and filling...watch them disappear!

32-oz. bag southern-style
    hash browns
2 c. sour cream

2 10-3/4 oz. cans cream of
    potato soup
4 c. shredded Cheddar cheese

Mix all ingredients together; pour in a lightly greased 13"x9" pan. Cover with aluminum foil; bake at 325 degrees for 2 hours, stirring occasionally. Makes 8 servings.

More diner lingo: Hand over Mike & Ike (salt & pepper).

Whistlin' Dixie
diner

Alabama-Style Pork Chops

Debra Donaldson
Florala, AL

Each time I make this dish, it brings back wonderful memories of cooking with Mama!

1/2 t. garlic powder
1/2 t. onion powder
1/2 t. dried rosemary
1/2 t. dried thyme
1/2 c. self-rising flour
6 center-cut pork chops
2 T. olive oil
10-3/4 oz. can cream of chicken soup
10-3/4-oz. can cream of celery soup
1/2 c. white wine
1/4 c. lemon-lime soda
1 onion, sliced thinly
1 red pepper, sliced
2 t. garlic, minced
salt and pepper to taste

Mix garlic powder, onion powder, rosemary, thyme and flour in a large plastic bag. Shake pork chops, one at a time, in the spices; brown in olive oil. In a separate mixing bowl, combine remaining ingredients. Layer pork chops in a 13"x9" lightly greased baking dish; pour soup mixture on top. Cover with aluminum foil; bake at 350 degrees for one hour. Uncover; cook an additional 35 to 45 minutes. Makes 6 servings.

For a sweet twist on a diner favorite, fill an old-fashioned chrome straw dispenser with licorice and candy sticks...what a treat!

Mustard Fried Catfish

Jennifer Petticoffer
Longview, TX

Throw on a side of fries and coleslaw and meet me in heaven!

8 catfish fillets
8-oz. jar mustard

7-oz. pkg. cornbread mix
oil for deep frying

Rinse catfish; pat dry. Brush with mustard; dip in cornbread mix. Heat 1/2 inch oil in a heavy skillet over medium-high heat; fry 3 minutes on each side or until fish is done. Serves 4.

New Orleans Rice

Carol Burns
Gooseberry Patch

This zesty rice comes straight from the bayou to you!

4 T. butter
1/2 c. onion, chopped
1/2 c. celery, chopped
1/2 c. green pepper, chopped
2 cloves garlic, minced

1/2 c. sliced mushrooms
1 c. instant rice, uncooked
salt to taste
1/2 t. cayenne pepper
2 c. beef broth

Melt butter in a saucepan; sauté onion, celery, green pepper, garlic and mushrooms until tender. Stir in rice; pour into a 2-quart casserole dish. Season with salt and cayenne pepper; add broth. Cover and bake at 350 degrees until liquid is absorbed, about 30 minutes. Makes 4 servings.

Good company in a journey makes the way seem shorter.
– Izaak Walton

Whistlin' Dixie
diner

Jambalaya

Jann Manwell
La Grande, OR

This hearty dish is delicious served with cornbread.

1 T. oil
1 onion, chopped
1/2 lb. turkey kielbasa, sliced
1/2 c. instant rice, uncooked
4 c. water
2 cubes chicken bouillon
16-oz. can pinto beans
15-1/2 oz. can black beans

14-1/2 oz. can diced tomatoes
1/2 t. dried oregano
1/2 t. dried thyme
1/2 t. pepper
2 t. cajun seasoning
1/4 lb. shrimp, peeled and
   cooked

Sauté onion and kielbasa in oil until onion is tender; add remaining ingredients. Bring to a boil; reduce heat and simmer 30 minutes. Makes 4 servings.

Oilcloth lends nostalgic charm to your tabletop and is a popular alternative to traditional tablecloths. It can be cut to measure and wipes clean with a damp cloth!

Hearty Pockets

Blanche Delay
Kamiah, ID

Stuffed full of goodness, they're great any time of day.

2 c. buttermilk biscuit mix
2 c. all-purpose flour
3/4 t. salt
1 c. margarine
water
1-1/2 lbs. ground beef, browned
    and drained

1 onion, chopped
2 carrots, coarsely grated
6 potatoes, peeled and diced
salt and pepper to taste
8 t. butter, divided

Combine biscuit mix, flour, salt and margarine together; add enough water to make a dough that can be rolled out. Divide into 8 balls; roll each out into a 6-inch circle. In a mixing bowl, combine ground beef, onion, carrot, potatoes, salt and pepper; spoon into center of each circle of dough. Dab one teaspoon butter on top of filling; fold over dough and pinch to seal edges. Bake at 350 degrees for one hour. Makes 8 servings.

Vintage metal picnic baskets, tin buckets and enamelware pails make handy carriers for all the fixin's for a picnic in the park!

Whistlin' Dixie
diner

Ham Loaf

Linda Abernethy
Mitchell, NE

Special enough for company and Sunday dinners too.

2 lbs. ground ham
1 lb. ground beef
1-1/2 c. cracker crumbs
2 eggs
1 c. milk

1/2 c. vinegar
1-1/2 c. brown sugar, packed
1/2 c. water
1 T. dry mustard

Combine ham, beef, cracker crumbs, eggs and milk; shape into 2 individual loaves and place in 9"x5" loaf pans. Mix remaining ingredients; pour over the loaves. Bake at 325 degrees for 1-1/2 hours; baste with juices occasionally during baking. Serves 12.

Zesty Hominy with Cheese

Shelly Boling
Artesia, NM

Great for potlucks...fast and tasty!

15-1/2 oz. can yellow hominy
4-oz. can green chilies
1 c. shredded Cheddar cheese

1-1/2 c. sour cream
1-1/2 c. instant rice, cooked

Combine ingredients together; pour into a 2-quart baking dish. Bake at 350 degrees for 30 to 45 minutes; cool. Serves 6.

Place old-fashioned sundae and parfait glasses in the freezer before using...sundaes, shakes and malts will stay cold & frosty longer!

Cornbread & Chicken Pie

Kristina Stewart
Waxahachie, TX

Add a can of green chilies for a spicy kick!

2 c. cooked chicken, diced
11-oz. can corn, drained
14-3/4 oz. can cream of mush-
    room soup
10-3/4 oz. can cream of broccoli
    soup

7-oz. box cornbread mix
1 egg, beaten
1/3 c. milk
Garnish: Cheddar cheese, grated

Combine chicken, corn and soups in a 9"x9" baking dish; smooth mixture with a spoon. In a separate bowl, mix cornbread, egg and milk until just moistened; pour over chicken mixture. Bake at 350 degrees for 30 to 35 minutes or until cornbread is golden. Makes 9 to 12 servings.

Part of the secret of success in life is to eat what you like and let the food fight it out inside!
– Mark Twain

Whistlin' Dixie
diner

Frosty Fruit Salad

Susan Biffignani
Fenton, MO

A chilly variation on a classic.

12-oz. can orange juice concentrate, thawed
5 to 6 bananas, sliced
20-oz. can crushed pineapple
20-oz. can sliced peaches

10-oz. pkg. frozen sliced strawberries
1-1/2 c. sugar
water

Prepare orange juice according to container directions in a large serving bowl; stir in bananas, crushed pineapple, peaches and strawberries, set aside. Add sugar and one cup water to a saucepan; bring to a boil. Pour over fruit; stir. Freeze 24 to 48 hours in a freezer-proof bowl; stir 2 to 3 times as it freezes. Serves 10 to 12.

You don't have to go to the diner for a rich, thick milkshake.
Mix hand-dipped ice cream, whole milk and hot fudge or fresh
strawberries in a blender, then top with whipped
cream and a cherry...enjoy!

Perfectly Pecan Pie

Alta Smith
Richmond, VA

THE southern tradition.

9-inch pie crust, unbaked
2 T. butter
1/2 c. sugar
2 eggs, beaten
2 T. all-purpose flour

1/4 t. salt
1 t. vanilla extract
1 c. corn syrup
1-1/2 c. chopped pecans

Line a pie pan with pie crust; set aside. Cream butter and sugar together; add eggs, flour, salt, vanilla and corn syrup, mixing well. Fold in pecans; pour into pie crust. Bake at 350 degrees for 45 to 50 minutes or until set. Cool and serve slightly warm. Makes 8 servings.

Candied Pecans

Beverly Mock
Pensacola, FL

Make lots...they'll be gone before you know it!

1 c. sugar
1/2 t. cinnamon
1/4 c. milk

2 T. water
1-1/2 c. pecans
1/2 t. vanilla extract

Combine sugar, cinnamon, milk and water together; cook until mixture reaches soft ball stage, 234 degrees on a candy thermometer. Remove from heat; stir in pecans and vanilla until mixture thickens. Spread pecans on wax paper to harden; store in an airtight container. Makes about one pound.

Add retro charm to your picnic by using one of your collectible salt & pepper sets or Bakelite-handled utensils.

Whistlin' Dixie
diner

Sour Cream-Peach Pie

Teressa McGuire
Greenville, OH

This pie is so delicious that my husband usually tries to keep the whole thing for himself!

29-oz. can sliced peaches,
   drained
2 9-inch pie crusts, unbaked
1 c. plus 2 T. sugar, divided

1 c. sour cream
5 T. all-purpose flour
1/4 t. salt
1/2 t. cinnamon

Pour peaches into bottom pie crust; set aside. Combine one cup sugar, sour cream, flour and salt; spread over peaches. In a small bowl, toss remaining sugar and cinnamon together; sprinkle on top. Place on top crust; bake at 450 degrees for 15 minutes; decrease oven temperature to 350 degrees and bake another 45 minutes. Makes 8 servings.

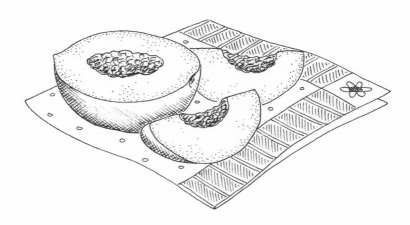

Look for unique travel souvenirs from vacation spots that can be used every day...pillow covers, paperweights, spoons and frosted tumblers are a great way to remember the fun-filled days of your vacation!

Strawberry Surprise Cake

Ellen Plutch
Marianna, PA

So refreshing with a tall glass of lemonade.

2 c. mini marshmallows
2 c. strawberries, sliced
3-oz. pkg. strawberry gelatin
2-1/2 c. all-purpose flour
1 c. sugar
1/2 c. shortening

3 t. baking powder
1/2 t. salt
1 c. milk
1 t. vanilla extract
3 eggs

Spread marshmallows on the bottom of a lightly greased 13"x9" pan; set aside. Combine strawberries and their juices with gelatin; set aside. Blend remaining ingredients; pour over marshmallows. Spoon strawberry mixture over the top. Bake at 350 degrees for 30 minutes; reduce heat to 300 degrees and continue baking for 15 minutes longer. Makes 15 servings.

My favorite thing is to go where I have never gone.
– Diane Arbus

Whistlin' Dixie
diner

Key Lime–White Chocolate Chippers

Cora Baker
La Rue, OH

*The perfect blend of sweet and citrus...try arranging them
in a small picnic basket lined with a pretty tablecloth
for a charming hostess gift.*

1/2 c. butter, softened
1 c. sugar
1 egg
1 egg yolk
1-1/2 c. all-purpose flour

1 t. baking powder
1/2 t. salt
1/4 c. lime juice
1-1/2 t. lime zest
3/4 c. white chocolate chips

Cream butter, sugar, egg and egg yolk in a large bowl; blend in flour, baking powder, salt, lime juice and lime zest. Fold in chocolate chips; roll dough into walnut-size balls. Place on ungreased baking sheets; bake at 350 degrees for 8 to 10 minutes. Makes 2-1/2 dozen.

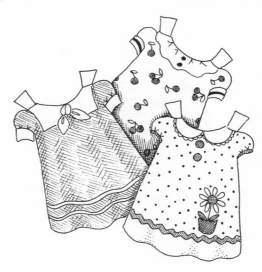

Decorate with pictures of the past! Make enlargements of vintage postcards or old ads to cover a tabletop or trunk...just protect with glass or clear polyurethane.

Pecan Pudding

Joyce Brown
Pensacola, FL

An old-fashioned favorite with the best of the south.

1 c. corn syrup
1/2 c. sugar
2 T. butter, melted
1 t. vanilla extract
3 eggs, beaten

1/2 c. all-purpose flour
1/8 t. cream of tartar
1 c. chopped pecans, divided
Garnish: powdered sugar

Add corn syrup, sugar, butter and vanilla to beaten eggs; mix well. In another bowl, sift flour with cream of tartar; add to egg mixture. Fold in 3/4 cup pecans; pour into a greased 10"x6" baking dish. Sprinkle remaining nuts over the top; bake at 375 degrees for 35 to 40 minutes. Spoon into dessert dishes; garnish with powdered sugar. Makes 6 to 8 servings.

Learn the names of stars and constellations so that when they shine above you, you'll be old friends.

Whistlin' Dixie
diner

Chocolate Chip Pie

Melissa Lawson
Alexandria, TN

*This recipe was passed to me from my aunt and has
always been a family favorite.*

1/2 c. all-purpose flour
1/2 c. sugar
1/2 c. brown sugar, packed
2 eggs, beaten

3/4 c. butter, softened
1 c. semi-sweet chocolate chips
1 c. chopped walnuts
9-inch pie crust, unbaked

Blend flour, sugar and brown sugar into eggs; add butter, mixing well.
Fold in chocolate chips and walnuts; pour into pie crust. Bake at
325 degrees for 55 to 60 minutes or until knife inserted into middle of
pie comes out clean. Serves 8.

**Use an old dish drainer to organize children's activity or
coloring books. The silverware holders can be used for
holding crayons, pencils or pens.**

Peach Cake

Lisa Ellsworth
Sparta, MO

Rich & creamy with a fruity surprise!

18-1/2 oz. pkg. yellow cake mix
3-1/2 oz. pkg. instant vanilla
   pudding
4 eggs
1 c. water

1 c. oil
29-oz. can sliced peaches,
   drained and juices reserved
1 c. sugar
8-oz. pkg. cream cheese

Combine cake mix, pudding, eggs, water and oil; pour into a lightly greased 13"x9" baking pan. Pour peaches over cake mix; set aside. Combine sugar, cream cheese and 5 tablespoons of reserved peach juice; beat until smooth. Pour over peaches; bake at 350 degrees for 50 minutes. Makes 12 to 15 servings.

Add some retro charm the next time you bake a Bundt® cake.
When serving, fill a vintage milk bottle with water and use it
to hold seasonal flowers in the center of the cake.

Whistlin' Dixie
diner

Orange Cream Fruit Salad

Karen Barineau
Aliso Viejo, CA

*Especially tasty in the summer but my family
requests it year 'round.*

3.4-oz. pkg. instant vanilla
   pudding
1-1/2 c. milk
1/3 c. orange juice concentrate,
   thawed
3/4 c. sour cream
20-oz. can pineapple tidbits,
   drained

15-oz. can sliced peaches,
   drained
11-oz. can mandarin oranges
2 bananas, sliced
1 apple, peeled, cored and sliced

Combine pudding mix, milk and orange juice in a medium mixing
bowl; beat with a mixer for 2 minutes on medium speed. Mix in sour
cream; set aside. Fold fruit together in a large serving bowl; gently mix
in sour cream mixture. Cover and refrigerate at least 2 hours. Makes
8 to 10 servings.

Happiness is a perfume you can't pour on others without
getting a few drops on yourself.
– Ralph Waldo Emerson

Monkey Paw Biscuits

Deborah Ellis
Fair Grove, MO

For as long as I can remember, my family has enjoyed these biscuits on Christmas morning with sparkling apple cider.

3/4 c. sugar
1/2 t. cinnamon
3 12-oz. cans refrigerated
   biscuits

1/4 c. evaporated milk
1/2 c. brown sugar, packed
3/4 c. butter

Combine sugar and cinnamon; set aside. Separate biscuits; cut each one into fourths. Coat with sugar and cinnamon mixture; stack in bottom and around sides of a lightly buttered Bundt® pan. Bring evaporated milk, brown sugar and butter to a boil in a small saucepan until thickened; pour over biscuits. Bake at 350 degrees for 35 minutes; cool slightly before removing from pan. Serve warm. Makes 12 servings.

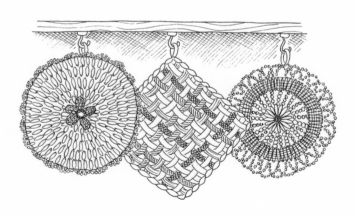

Add a retro flair to your kitchen with crocheted potholders, doilies, vintage napkins and tablecloths...quick & easy!

Whistlin' Dixie
diner

Pecan Pie Muffins

Karrie Middaugh
Superior Township, MI

Who says you can't have pie for breakfast?

1 c. brown sugar, packed
1/2 c. all-purpose flour
1 c. chopped pecans

2/3 c. butter, softened
2 eggs, beaten

Combine brown sugar, flour and pecans together in a medium mixing bowl; set aside. Blend butter and eggs together in a separate bowl until creamy; stir into dry ingredients until just combined. Spoon batter into 18 greased and floured mini muffin cups; bake at 350 degrees for 20 to 25 minutes. Cool on wire racks. Makes 1-1/2 dozen.

Use a muffin tin on your desktop to corral paperclips,
tacks and rubberbands. A fun way to
keep everything handy!

Molasses Cookies

Jennifer Lanza
Frisco, TX

*The smell of these cookies baking reminds me of home
and Grandma's warm kitchen.*

4 c. all-purpose flour
2 t. baking soda
2 t. cinnamon
1 t. ground ginger
2 t. ground cloves

1 t. salt
2 c. sugar
1-1/2 c. butter
2 eggs
1/2 c. molasses

Combine flour, baking soda, cinnamon, ginger, cloves and salt in a
medium bowl; set aside. Cream sugar and butter together in a large
mixing bowl; add eggs and molasses, mixing well. Gradually add in
flour mixture; roll dough into one-inch balls. Place on ungreased
baking sheets; flatten with the bottom of a glass that has been dipped
in butter and then sugar to achieve 1/4-inch thickness. Bake at
375 degrees for 8 to 10 minutes. Makes about 6 dozen.

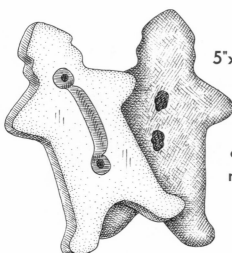

Make some
5"x7" enlargements of your
vacation photos, place in
frames and decorate
your walls with a cluster
of prized travel shots...a
mini vacation every time
you see them!

CACTUS

Slim's

Pull up a chair for some Tex-Mex fare.

Slim's Cinnamon Blitz

Lisa Johnson
Hallsville, TX

*Start your day with these cream cheese roll-ups
touched with cinnamon...delicious!*

2 loaves white bread
8-oz. pkg. cream cheese,
  softened

1/2 c. butter, melted
cinnamon and sugar to taste

Remove crusts from bread; flatten each slice with a rolling pin. Spread a thin layer of cream cheese over each slice; roll up jelly roll-style. Cut each roll in half; coat with melted butter. Sprinkle with cinnamon and sugar mixture; place on an ungreased baking sheet. Bake at 350 degrees for 10 minutes. Makes about 2 to 3 dozen.

"Are we there yet?" Let children follow the trip on a map so they can see the progress you're making.

150

CACTUS
Slim's

Fry Bread

Ann Gooch
Round Rock, TX

*For a new breakfast twist, try fry bread and gravy
instead of biscuits & gravy.*

1 c. all-purpose flour
1/2 t. baking powder
salt and pepper to taste

1/2 c. milk
oil for deep-frying

Combine flour, baking powder, salt and pepper; slowly add milk until dough becomes smooth and elastic. Drop dough by tablespoonfuls into a heavy pan filled with a one-inch depth of heated oil. Dough should double in bulk. Remove when golden brown on both sides; drain. Makes about 10.

Roasted Ear Hotcakes

Sallyann Steele
Tyrone, PA

Sprinkle with powdered sugar or spread with your favorite jam.

2 ears corn, roasted
4 eggs, beaten
1 c. all-purpose flour
1 c. cornmeal
1 t. baking soda

1 t. baking powder
1 t. salt
1 T. butter, melted
1-1/2 c. buttermilk

Remove corn from cobs, discarding cobs; combine with remaining ingredients. Drop by heaping tablespoonfuls onto a well-greased hot skillet; turn to brown both sides evenly. Makes 12 servings.

**For a diner-style dessert, pile gelatin cubes into a
dessert cup and top with a dollop of whipped cream
and a cherry...very sweet and refreshing!**

10–Gallon Hash

Wendy Lee Paffenroth
Pine Island, NY

Top with a fried egg for a spicy breakfast treat.

1-1/2 lb. ground beef, browned
2 to 3 c. onions, sliced
1 green pepper, thinly sliced
1/8 t. garlic powder
2 t. chili powder

salt and pepper to taste
14-1/2 oz. can stewed tomatoes
1 c. water
3/4 c. instant rice, uncooked

Combine all ingredients except rice in a large skillet; bring to a boil, stirring often. Add rice; cover and remove from heat. Let stand until rice is tender, about 5 minutes. Makes 4 servings.

A man travels the world over in search of
what he needs, and returns home to find it.
– George Moore

CACTUS
Slim's

Apple Enchiladas

Flo Burtnett
Gage, OK

Enjoy these enchiladas for breakfast or as a yummy dessert!

21-oz. can apple pie filling
6 8-inch flour tortillas
1 t. cinnamon
1/3 c. margarine

1/2 c. sugar
1/2 c. brown sugar, packed
1/2 c. water

Spoon apple filling evenly down center of each tortilla; sprinkle with cinnamon. Roll up; place, seam side down, in a lightly greased 2-quart baking dish. In a medium saucepan, bring margarine, sugars and water to a boil; reduce heat and simmer for 3 minutes, stirring constantly. Pour over enchiladas; let stand 30 minutes. Bake at 350 degrees for 20 minutes. Makes 6 servings.

Have a cup of coffee and listen to some diner music.
Suggestions include "Chantilly Lace," "In the Still of the Night,"
"Who Put the Bomp" and "Do Wah Diddy Diddy."

Sopapillas

Linda Eldridge
Santa Teresa, NM

For even more sweetness, serve with a dish of honey for dipping.

2 T. active dry yeast
1/4 c. plus 2 t. sugar, divided
2 c. warm water, divided
3 t. salt
3 T. shortening

1 egg
5 c. all-purpose flour
oil for deep-frying
Garnish: sugar and cinnamon

Sprinkle yeast and 1/2 teaspoon sugar over 1/2 cup warm water; set aside 5 minutes. Mix yeast mixture with remaining ingredients excluding oil; knead lightly. Place dough in a lightly greased mixing bowl; cover and let rise for 45 minutes. Divide dough in half; roll out to pie crust thinness. Cut dough into squares; deep-fry in hot oil until golden brown. Drain on paper towels; sprinkle with cinnamon and sugar. Makes 2 dozen.

Just for fun, play "Waiter and Waitress" and let the kids help out in the kitchen...Mom & Dad can be the customers!

CACTUS
Slim's

Rise & Shine Torte

Sue Cherry
Starkville, MS

A hearty breakfast with Tex-Mex flair the whole family will love.

2 eggs, beaten
1/2 t. salt
2 T. all-purpose flour
1/3 c. milk
4-oz. can diced green chilies

1 c. sharp Cheddar cheese, grated
1 c. Monterey Jack cheese, grated

Combine eggs, salt, flour, and milk; mix well. Add remaining ingredients, mixing well. Pour into a well-greased 13"x9" baking pan; bake at 350 degrees for 35 minutes. Cut into small squares to serve. Makes 2 dozen servings.

Travel tip: use serving trays in the car for crafting, puzzles, board games or Play-Doh.

Jalapeño Poppers

Kelly Knower
Ringoes, NJ

Add a little spice to your life with these
cheesy snacks...they're a sure-fire hit!

24 pickled jalapeño peppers
1 lb. Cheddar cheese
1/2 c. cornmeal
1/2 c. all-purpose flour

1 t. salt
2 eggs, beaten
oil for deep-frying

Make a short slit into each jalapeño pepper; remove as many seeds as possible. Slice cheese into strips 1/4" wide and one-inch long; lay one in each jalapeño. Combine cornmeal, flour and salt in a small mixing bowl; place beaten eggs in a separate bowl. Dip peppers into egg mixture; roll in cornmeal mixture until well-coated. Set aside on a wire rack for 1/2 hour; deep-fry in 375-degree oil in small batches until crisp and golden, about 4 minutes. Remove using a slotted spoon; drain on paper towels. Makes 2 dozen.

Visit a giant meteor crater, lava fields and Indian ruins in Flagstaff, Arizona. Take in a view at the Lowell Observatory where the planet Pluto was discovered in 1932.

CACTUS
Slim's

Spicy Guacamole

Sharon Reagan
Concord, NH

Grab the nachos, tortilla chips, pita chips, veggies, pretzels...dip in!

4 avocados, peeled and chopped
1 clove garlic, minced
2 T. lemon juice
1 t. pepper

1 tomato, diced
1/8 t. cayenne pepper

Mash avocados with a fork; stir in remaining ingredients. Makes about 2 cups.

Black & White Salsa

Kristen Halverson
Folsom, CA

This salsa looks as great as it tastes.

10-oz. pkg. shoe peg frozen
    corn, partially thawed
15-1/2 oz. can black beans,
    rinsed and drained
1 bunch green onions, diced
1 red tomato, diced
1 yellow tomato, diced

juice of 2 limes
1 jalapeño pepper, diced
1 T. olive oil
1/2 t. salt
1/8 t. pepper
fresh cilantro, chopped, to taste

Combine corn, beans, onion and tomatoes together; set aside. Mix remaining ingredients together; combine mixtures before serving. Makes 3 to 4 cups.

Certainly, travel is more than the seeing of sights;

it is a change that goes on, deep and permanent,

in the ideas of living.

– Miriam Beard

Sun-Dried Tomato Salsa

Angela Murphy
Tempe, AZ

For an extra smoky taste, roast tomatoes, pepper and garlic
before adding to salsa.

4-oz. pkg. morel mushrooms
3 T. olive oil, divided
1/2 c. onion, diced
3 Roma tomatoes
1 c. sun-dried tomatoes in oil,
   diced
3 T. red bell pepper, seeded and
   diced

3 cloves garlic, minced
2 T. fresh parsley, minced
1 T. balsamic vinegar
1 t. garlic salt
1/2 t. pepper
2 T. lemon juice

Brush mushrooms with one tablespoon oil; grill until tender. Dice;
set aside. Sauté onion in one tablespoon oil for 5 minutes; add to
mushroom mixture. Slice tomatoes; squeeze and discard seeds and
juice. Chop solids; add to mushroom mix. Fold in remaining
ingredients; combine thoroughly. Makes about 2 cups.

**Decorate a kitchen wall by framing colorful advertisements of
your favorite products from vintage magazines.**

CACTUS
Slim's

Longhorn Caviar

Jo Ann

*Add more jalapeño for extra heat and serve
with crisp tortilla chips.*

1-1/2 c. tomatoes, seeded and
  chopped
1/3 c. green onions, sliced
3 T. green chilies, diced
2 T. white vinegar
1 T. jalapeño pepper, seeded and
  minced
1-1/2 T. fresh cilantro, chopped
2 t. olive oil

1/4 t. garlic salt
1/4 t. cumin
1/8 t. pepper
2 cloves garlic, minced
15.8-oz. can black-eyed peas,
  drained
Garnish: jalapeño slices and
  cilantro sprigs

Stir first 12 ingredients together; cover and chill. Add garnishes to
bowl before serving. Makes 3-1/2 cups.

Make an "Our Vacation" collage! Include photos, pamphlets,
ticket stubs and postcards on a corkboard or paste onto
poster board and frame so you'll remember all the fun.

Nacho Dip

Debbie Patrick
Kingston, OH

*For a colorful display, serve with yellow, blue and white
corn tortillas chips.*

2 8-oz. pkgs. cream cheese,
   softened
1 c. sour cream
1-1/4 oz. pkg. taco seasoning

8-oz. jar salsa
8-oz. pkg. shredded Cheddar
   cheese

Blend cream cheese, sour cream and taco seasoning together; pour
into a 9" pie plate. Spread salsa over the top; sprinkle with cheese.
Makes 4 cups.

Kwik Korn Chip Dip

Lori Vernon
Centralia, KS

Also yummy as a topping for burritos and enchiladas.

11-oz. can sweet corn and diced
   peppers, drained
14-1/2-oz. can tomatoes with
   green chile peppers

8-oz. pkg. shredded Cheddar
   cheese
1 c. sour cream
6 to 10 green onions, sliced

Combine all ingredients together; refrigerate at least one hour. Makes
5 cups.

Search your favorite shops for early plastic radios!
They make whimsical retro accents in your home
and come in an array of vintage colors.

CACTUS
Slim's

Chicken-Swiss Enchiladas

Angie Keyes
E. Lansing, MI

*This quick & easy meal is great for those days when
you don't have a lot of time to cook.*

1 c. sour cream
4-oz. can green chilies
10-3/4 oz. can cream of chicken
   soup

2 chicken breasts, cooked and
   shredded
6-oz. pkg. Swiss cheese slices
10-1/2 oz. pkg. flour tortillas

Blend sour cream, green chilies and cream of chicken soup together;
pour 1/2 on bottom of a 13"x9" baking dish. Divide shredded chicken
and Swiss cheese among tortillas; roll each and place on sauce. Top
with remaining soup mixture; bake at 350 degrees for 30 minutes.
Makes 12.

To look, really look, out in the world as it is framed
in the window of a moving vehicle, is to become a child again.
– Unknown

Taco Sauce

Tina Knotts
Gooseberry Patch

*This tasty recipe can be used as a sauce or topping for any
Tex-Mex recipe...great as a dip too.*

1 onion, diced
1 green pepper, diced
1 T. oil
1 red chili, seeded and chopped
1/2 t. cumin
1/2 T. fresh cilantro, minced

1 clove garlic, pressed
salt and pepper to taste
1/8 t. sugar
14-oz. can tomatoes
tomato paste for thickening

Sauté onion and pepper in oil until tender; add chili, cumin, cilantro
and garlic. Cook for 2 to 3 minutes. Mix in salt, pepper, sugar and
tomatoes; heat 4 to 6 minutes over moderate heat or until thickened.
Add tomato paste to reach desired consistency. Makes about 2 cups.

Give your make-ahead meals a new twist. Dish them into
divided plates, cover with foil when reheating to recall TV
dinners...they first appeared in the 1950's.

CACTUS
Slim's

Baked Cowboy Dip

Lisa Bakovic
Franklin, WI

Serve with loads of fresh veggies and toasted bread cubes.

1 round loaf sourdough or
    pumpernickel bread
8-oz. pkg. cream cheese,
    softened

1/2 c. sour cream
1/4 c. salsa
1-1/2 c. shredded Cheddar
    cheese

Remove 1/4-inch slice from top of the bread loaf; set aside. Scoop out center of bread leaving a 1/2-inch thick shell; cube removed bread. Toast cubed bread in 400 degree oven, about 5 minutes; set aside. Blend cream cheese, sour cream and salsa until smooth; stir in Cheddar cheese. Spoon into bread shell; place reserved slice on top. Wrap in aluminum foil; bake for 45 to 60 minutes. Serve warm. Makes 2 cups.

How many different license plates can you spot in one road trip? Keep a list of the ones you see...write down the state, color and any special designs or words you notice on them.

Ham Rolls

Alma Krueger
Costa Mesa, CA

These rolls are great reheated for lunch the next day.

12 thin slices ham
12 thin slices Swiss cheese
2 10-oz. pkgs. frozen broccoli,
    cooked and drained

2.8-oz. can French fried onions

Layer one slice ham, one slice Swiss cheese and one tablespoon of broccoli; roll up and place in a 13"x9" baking pan. Repeat with all ham slices. Pour 2 cups white sauce over the ham rolls; sprinkle with French fried onions. Bake at 350 degrees for 20 minutes. Makes 12 servings.

White Sauce:

4 T. butter
4 T. all-purpose flour

1/4 t. salt
2 c. milk

Melt butter in saucepan over low heat; blend in flour and salt. Add milk all at once; cook quickly, stirring constantly until mixture thickens and bubbles.

Travel tip: Play Oshkosh! Pick a category such as mailboxes, fire hydrants or public telephones...the first person to spot one calls out, "Oshkosh!" and receives one point. The first player to reach 15 points wins.

CACTUS
Slim's

Round-Up Green Beans

Lucinda Lewis
Brownstown, IN

*Make a day or two ahead of time and store in the fridge
until ready to serve.*

1 c. catsup
1 T. Worcestershire sauce
1 c. brown sugar, packed
4 14-1/2 oz. cans green beans,
    drained

6 slices bacon, diced
1 onion, chopped
salt and pepper to taste

Combine catsup, Worcestershire sauce and brown sugar together; toss
with green beans and set aside. Sauté bacon and onion until bacon is
crisp; drain and add to beans. Salt and pepper to taste; pour into a
greased 2-quart baking dish. Cover and bake at 325 degrees for
3 hours. Makes 12 to 16 servings.

Search flea markets for vintage decals from gas stations,
states and motels...have fun putting them in a window,
on a mirror or on your car!

Chunky Tomato–Pasta Bake

Jewel Sharpe
Raleigh, NC

With only five ingredients, this dish is so easy to make...you can whip it up in a jiffy!

6-oz. pkg. rigatoni, cooked and drained
1 lb. ground beef, browned
14-oz. can diced seasoned tomatoes with green pepper and onion

10-3/4 oz. can cream of mushroom soup
1-1/2 c. shredded mozzarella cheese

Combine pasta, meat, tomatoes and soup in a lightly greased 11"x7" baking dish. Cover and bake at 350 degrees for 25 minutes; uncover and top with cheese. Bake until cheese melts. Makes 4 servings.

When cooking spaghetti, add a pat of butter or a few teaspoons of cooking oil to prevent pasta from sticking together.

CACTUS
Slim's

Chicken Marimba

Kristine Marumoto
Sandy, UT

Everyone loves this cheesy casserole...it's a potluck favorite!

1/2 c. onion, chopped
1/2 c. green pepper, chopped
1 c. sliced mushrooms
2 T. butter
10-3/4 oz. can cream of chicken
  soup
1/3 c. milk
1/4 c. pimento, chopped

1/2 t. dried basil
4 oz. bowtie pasta, cooked and
  drained
1-1/2 c. cottage cheese
3 c. cooked chicken, diced
2 c. shredded Cheddar cheese
1/2 c. fresh Parmesan cheese,
  grated

Sauté onions, pepper and mushrooms in butter until tender; stir in soup, milk, pimento and basil. Layer half the noodles and half the soup mixture in bottom of a 13"x9" baking pan. Blend cottage cheese until smooth; spread half over noodles and soup. Add layer of half the cooked chicken, half the Cheddar cheese and half the Parmesan cheese. Repeat layers. Bake at 350 degrees for 45 minutes to one hour. Serves 6 to 8.

License plates had distinct sizes and shapes in the 1950's...look for license plates from different states at flea markets. Nail them up in a garage, shed or back porch for a touch of vintage charm.

x

Supper in a Flash

Monica Talley
San Antonio, TX

*This is a favorite recipe of mine because I can have it
on the table in under 30 minutes.*

3 cloves garlic, minced
1/2 c. sliced mushrooms
2 T. olive oil
14-1/2 oz. can peeled diced
   tomatoes
15-1/2 oz. can Great Northern
   beans, rinsed and drained

1/16 t. red pepper flakes
6 fresh basil leaves, chopped
8-oz. box penne pasta, cooked
   and drained
1/2 t. salt
1/4 t. pepper

Sauté garlic and mushrooms in oil for one minute; add tomatoes, beans and red pepper flakes. Heat until boiling; return to a simmer. Add basil and pasta; season with salt and pepper. Serves 4.

A vacation is having nothing to do and all day to do it in.
– Robert Orben

CACTUS
Slim's

Jalapeño Cornbread

Alice Ketchersid
Bloomington, IN

Whip up some of this spicy cornbread for your next fiesta!

1 c. cornmeal
3 T. all-purpose flour
2 t. baking powder
1/2 t. salt

1 egg
14-3/4 oz. can creamed corn
2 jalapeño peppers, seeded and
   chopped

Combine ingredients together; pour into greased muffin pans. Bake at 450 degrees for 25 to 30 minutes. Makes about 12 servings.

Southwestern Squares

Karla Nitz
Janesville, WI

Serve with crackers or tortilla chips.

8-oz. pkg. sharp Cheddar
   cheese, grated and divided
4-oz. can diced jalapeño
   peppers, drained
2 c. sour cream, divided
8-oz. pkg. mild Cheddar cheese,
   grated and divided

8-oz. pkg. Monterey Jack cheese,
   grated
4-oz. can diced green chilies,
   drained
2 green onions, diced

Layer ingredients in a lightly greased 8"x8" baking pan in the following order: 1/2 cup sharp Cheddar, jalapeño peppers, one cup sour cream, 1/2 cup mild Cheddar, 1/2 cup Monterey Jack, remaining sharp Cheddar, green chilies, remaining sour cream, mild Cheddar and Monterey Jack. Sprinkle the top with green onions; bake at 375 degrees for 30 minutes or until center is set. Cut into squares to serve. Makes 4 dozen.

Chicken Pizza Puff

Tracey Monnette
Roseville, MI

Serve with additional salsa on the side for dipping.

1 loaf frozen bread dough,
    thawed
2 chicken breasts, cooked and
    cubed

1/2 c. salsa
1/2 c. shredded mozzarella
    cheese

Divide thawed dough into 8 equal pieces; roll each piece into a
1/4-inch thick rectangle. Spoon chicken, salsa and cheese into the
middle of each rectangle; fold dough over and pinch sides to seal.
Allow to rise for 30 minutes; bake at 400 degrees for 15 minutes or
until golden brown. Makes 8 servings.

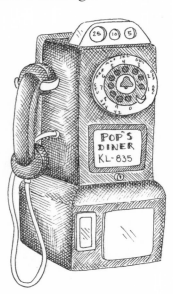

Invite friends over for a night of movie memories from the
1950's. Rent movies like *Roman Holiday*, *Giant*, *The Band
Wagon* or *Bedtime for Bonzo*...top it off with
hot, crispy popcorn and ice-cold cherry colas.

CACTUS
Slim's

Corn Sesame Sauté

Ellen LaRose
Littleton, NH

The perfect side for grilled chicken or steak.

3 T. butter
1 clove garlic, minced
2 T. sesame seed
3 T. green pepper, chopped
3 T. red pepper, chopped

1/2 t. salt
1/4 t. fresh basil, chopped
1/8 t. pepper
10-oz. pkg. frozen corn, cooked
and drained

Heat all ingredients except corn in a large saucepan for 5 minutes; add corn and heat through. Makes 6 servings.

Stewed Veggies

Jennifer Westerman
Osawatomie, KS

Yummy over noodles or served up as a side!

4 tomatoes, stewed
1 zucchini, sliced
2 carrots, sliced
1 cucumber, sliced

1/2 onion, chopped
3 T. sugar
salt and pepper to taste
1 T. butter

Combine ingredients in a saucepan; let simmer until vegetables are tender. Makes 4 servings.

Treat your family and guests to diner-style milkshakes using a selection of ice cream and syrups. Simply mix with whole milk in a blender and serve in tall glasses topped with whipped cream, cherries and a colorful straw...but they'll probably need a spoon!

Red Bandanna Stew

Doni Boothe
Magnolia, TX

A slow cooker makes this dish a low-fuss meal for families on the go.

1 lb. ground beef, browned
2 15-oz. cans new potatoes, drained and chopped
8-1/4 oz. can sliced carrots, drained

1-1/4 oz. pkg. taco seasoning mix
1/2 c. water
1 c. picante sauce
1 c. Cheddar cheese, grated

Place browned beef in a slow cooker; add potatoes and carrots. In a separate mixing bowl, combine taco seasoning with water; pour into slow cooker. Cook on high setting about 30 minutes to one hour; garnish with picante sauce and cheese. Serves 4 to 6.

From there to here, from here to there,
funny things are everywhere!
– Dr. Seuss

CACTUS
Slim's

Ranch Soup

Kristina Stewart
Waxahachie, TX

Serve with garlic toast for a super-fast dinner.

1 onion, chopped
1 lb. ground beef, browned
15-oz. can ranch-style beans
10-1/2 oz. can vegetable soup

1 c. salsa
1 c. elbow macaroni, cooked and
   drained

Add onion to browned beef; sauté until tender. Pour in beans, soup, salsa and macaroni; bring to a boil. Reduce heat; simmer 15 minutes. Makes 4 servings.

Decorate a baby boomer birthday cake with a trinket from the
past...a perfect topping may be a Barbie doll
or a Hot Wheels car!

Desert Chicken-Brown Rice

Mona Fagerwick
Fargo, ND

*The cooked, seasoned chicken in this dish is also tasty
in tacos and burritos.*

1-1/2 lbs. chicken breasts,
  chopped
1 t. chili powder
1 t. cumin
2 cloves garlic, minced
1/4 c. onion, minced
1 T. olive oil
15-oz. can diced tomatoes,
  drained, juice reserved

1/4 c. salsa
1 c. instant brown rice,
  uncooked
15-oz. can kidney beans,
  drained and rinsed
1/2 c. shredded Monterey Jack
  cheese

Brown chicken, spices, garlic and onion in olive oil; drain. Add water
to reserved tomato juice to make 2-1/4 cups liquid; pour over cooked
chicken. Add salsa; mix well. Stir in rice; cover and heat 5 minutes or
until liquid is absorbed. Add tomatoes and kidney beans; heat 5 more
minutes. Sprinkle cheese on top; cover and let simmer until cheese is
melted. Makes 4 to 6 servings.

For long road trips, write down the names of
your children's favorite songs on separate pieces of paper.
Take turns pulling one piece of paper out of a container
to decide what song to sing next.

CACTUS
Slim's

Aztec Casserole

Jenny Rubart
Holladay, UT

*Try serving this dish with shredded lettuce
and fresh, diced tomatoes.*

9 6-inch corn tortillas, halved
2 10-oz. cans enchilada sauce
1-1/2 to 2 c. sour cream
2 c. shredded Cheddar cheese,
   divided

1 c. salsa
1 c. canned corn
1 lb. boneless skinless chicken
   breasts, cooked and cubed

Dip 9 tortilla halves in enchilada sauce; arrange in bottom of a lightly greased 13"x9" baking pan and set aside. Combine sour cream, one cup cheese, salsa, corn and chicken; mix well. Spread half of chicken mixture over tortilla halves; repeat layer of remaining tortilla halves and chicken mixture. Sprinkle with remaining cheese; bake at 350 degrees for 25 to 30 minutes. Makes 6 to 8 servings.

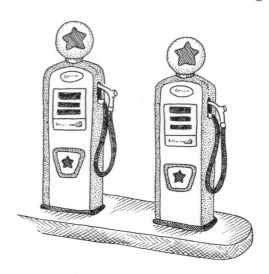

**A traveler without observation is a bird without wings.
– Moslih Eddin Saadi**

Chili Ranch Casserole

Barbara Stroud
Dennis, TX

Packed with peppers, this yummy casserole is delicious served with warm, homemade bread.

1 red pepper, chopped
1 green pepper, chopped
1 yellow pepper, chopped
1/2 c. onion, chopped
2 T. olive oil

1 lb. ground beef, browned
8-oz. can tomato sauce
1 t. chili powder
1 c. instant rice, cooked
15-oz. can ranch-style beans

Sauté peppers and onion in olive oil until tender; drain. Add beef, tomato sauce, chili powder and rice; simmer for 1/2 hour. Stir in beans; simmer 5 more minutes or until warmed thoroughly. Makes 4 servings.

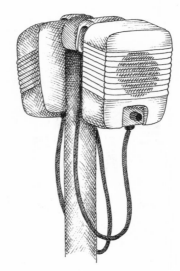

To travel hopefully is a better thing than to arrive.
– Robert Louis Stevenson

CACTUS
Slim's

Horseradish-Potatoes

Lucinda Lewis
Brownstown, IN

My family loves these potatoes served with pork roast.

3 c. instant potato flakes
8-oz. pkg. cream cheese
2 c. sour cream

5-oz. jar horseradish
2 T. butter

Cook potatoes according to package directions; set aside. Mix cream cheese, sour cream and horseradish together until smooth and creamy; fold in potatoes. Pour into a 2-quart greased baking dish; dot with butter. Bake, uncovered, at 350 degrees for 30 to 40 minutes. Makes 12 servings.

Beefy Beans

Kathy Crane
Gulf Breeze, FL

This dish can also be prepared in a slow cooker on low for an hour or two.

2-lb. can pork and beans
1 lb. ground beef, browned
12-oz. jar chili sauce

2 T. brown sugar, packed
1 onion, diced
salt and pepper to taste

Combine ingredients; pour into a greased 2-quart baking dish. Bake at 350 degrees for 30 minutes. Serves 4 to 6.

Diner Lingo: Order mashed potatoes
"in the alley"...served as a side dish.

Cornbread Salad

Sue Alley
Fredericktown, MO

*A new twist on an old favorite...your family
will request it year 'round.*

7-oz. pkg. cornbread mix, baked
8 slices bacon, crisply cooked
   and crumbled
1 tomato, diced
1 green pepper, diced

1 bunch green onions, sliced
1 c. mayonnaise-type salad
   dressing
1/4 c. sugar
1/4 c. sweet pickle juice

Crumble cornbread; set aside. Toss tomato, green pepper and onion
together; set aside. Whisk dressing, sugar and pickle juice together; set
aside. Just before serving, mix cornbread, bacon and vegetables
together; pour dressing on top. Toss well; serve immediately.
Serves 6.

**A crisp, frilly, bib apron hanging on a hook in your kitchen is
a fun accent and will remind you of simpler days.**

CACTUS
Slim's

Mexican Lasagna

Karen Larson
St. Louis, MO

This is delicious served with sour cream and salsa.

10 flour tortillas, quartered
1 lb. ground beef, browned
1 c. salsa
15-oz. can tomato sauce
1-1/4 oz. pkg. taco seasoning

16-oz. carton cottage cheese
1 T. dried oregano
2 eggs, beaten
1-1/2 c. mozzarella cheese

Layer 1/2 of tortilla quarters on bottom of a lightly greased
13"x9" baking dish; set aside. Combine ground beef, salsa, tomato
sauce and taco seasoning together; layer half on tortillas. In a separate
mixing bowl, combine cottage cheese, oregano and beaten eggs; layer
over meat mixture. Spread remaining meat mixture on top; layer
remaining tortilla quarters over meat mixture. Sprinkle with mozzarella
cheese; bake at 375 degrees for 30 minutes. Makes 12 servings.

Flour Tortillas

Janey Davila
La Habra, CA

Fresh, warm tortillas are the perfect addition to any Tex-Mex meal.

3 c. all-purpose flour
5 t. salt
1 t. baking powder

1/3 c. oil
2 c. hot water

Combine flour, salt and baking powder together; add oil, mix well.
Gradually stir in water in small amounts until dough forms; knead for
5 minutes. Divide dough into one tablespoon amounts; roll out thinly
into an 8-inch circle. Cook on non-stick griddle until golden on each
side; flipping once. Makes about 18 tortillas.

Taco Salad

Lisa McMorrow
Phoenix, AZ

I serve this salad at all of our get-togethers.

1 lb. ground beef, browned
1-1/4 oz. pkg. taco seasoning
1 head lettuce, torn
12 cherry tomatoes, quartered

2 c. shredded Cheddar cheese
6-oz. can sliced olives, drained
8-oz. bottle French dressing
15-1/2 oz. bag tortilla chips

Prepare ground beef with taco seasoning according to package directions; set aside to cool. Toss lettuce, tomatoes, and cheese together; add meat mixture, olives and French dressing. Place in refrigerator to blend flavors, at least one hour. Before serving, crush tortilla chips and add to the salad; mix well. Serves 6 to 8.

A diner-themed dinner is fun for the whole family...make place mats from vintage maps, roll up flatware in paper napkins and serve ketchup & mustard from plastic squeeze bottles.

CACTUS
Slim's

South of the Border Quiche

Valerie Neeley
Robinson, IL

You can serve this hearty pie any time of day!

1/2 lb. ground beef
1/4 c. onion, chopped
1-1/4 oz. pkg. taco seasoning
9-inch pie crust, baked
4 T. green chilies
2 c. shredded Monterey Jack
   cheese

3 eggs, beaten
1 c. milk
1/4 t. salt
1/8 t. garlic powder
1 c. lettuce, shredded
1/2 c. tomatoes, chopped
1/3 c. sour cream

Brown ground beef and onion; drain. Mix in half of the taco seasoning; save remaining for another recipe. Spoon mixture into pie crust. Add green chilies and cheese; set aside. Combine eggs, milk, salt and garlic powder together in a separate mixing bowl; pour over meat mixture. Bake at 375 degrees for 35 to 40 minutes; top with shredded lettuce and tomatoes. Dot with sour cream. Makes 8 servings.

Use tiles to lay a cheery black & white checkerboard pattern on your countertops and backsplash...very retro!

Zesty Salsa & Cheese Bread

Cheryl Wilson
Coshocton, OH

This is one of my favorite family recipes...enjoy!

10-oz. tube refrigerated pizza
   crust
8-oz. jar salsa
garlic salt to taste

8-oz. pkg. shredded Cheddar
   cheese
8-oz. pkg. shredded mozzarella
   cheese

Spread pizza crust on lightly greased baking sheet. Spread salsa down the middle of the pizza crust. Sprinkle salsa with garlic salt and cheeses. Bring edges of pizza crust to middle, leaving approximately one inch open. Bake at 375 degrees for 15 to 20 minutes or until cheese is melted and crust is golden brown. Slice and serve warm. Serves 4.

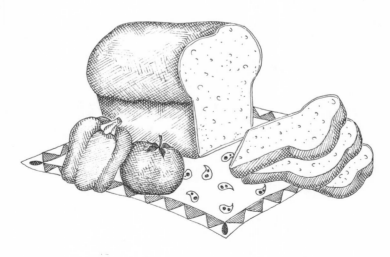

Remember your favorite childhood toys? Many can still be shared with kids today...Mr. Potato Head, Silly Putty, Slinky and Lincoln Logs are fun no matter what your age.

CACTUS
Slim's

3-Pepper Quesadillas

Michelle Serrano
Ramona, CA

This is a great appetizer or a light dinner served with a salad.

1 green pepper, thinly sliced
1 red pepper, thinly sliced
1 yellow pepper, thinly sliced
1/2 onion, thinly sliced
1/3 c. margarine
1/2 t. cumin
8-oz. pkg. cream cheese,
  softened

8-oz. pkg. shredded sharp
  Cheddar cheese
1/2 c. fresh Parmesan cheese,
  grated
10 6-inch flour tortillas

Sauté peppers and onions in margarine in a 12-inch skillet until tender; stir in cumin. Drain; reserve drippings. Blend cheeses on medium speed in a small mixing bowl until well mixed; spoon 2 tablespoons cheese mixture onto each tortilla. Top with pepper mixture; fold tortillas in half and place on a baking sheet. Brush tops with reserved drippings; bake at 425 degrees for 10 minutes. Slice each tortilla into thirds. Makes 30 servings.

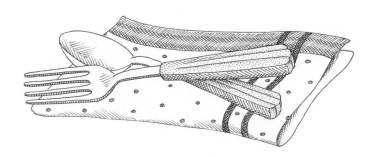

Did you know that some diners would determine the price of the Blue Plate Special by popping a balloon containing a tiny piece of paper with prices ranging from a penny to 25 cents?

Fried Ice Cream

Christy Chadwell
Wimberley, TX

The perfect way to cool down after a spicy Tex-Mex meal.

1/4 c. butter
1/2 c. sugar
2 c. corn flake cereal, crushed

2 scoops vanilla ice cream
Garnish: whipped topping and
  cherries

Melt butter and sugar in a saucepan until dissolved; remove from heat and stir in crushed corn flakes. Spread mixture onto parchment paper; roll scoops of ice cream in crumb mixture until covered. Place into freezer for one hour; top with whipped topping and cherry before serving. Makes 2 servings.

Browse flea markets for vintage, footed dessert dishes...they're a delightful retro-style way to serve ice cream and pudding.

CACTUS
Slim's

Lasso Cake

Neta Liebscher
El Reno, OK

You don't need a Texas-size appetite to enjoy this yummy cake!

2 c. all-purpose flour
2 t. baking soda
20-oz. can pineapple tidbits,
   drained

2 c. sugar
2 eggs, beaten
1 c. chopped pecans

Blend ingredients together; mix well. Pour into a lightly greased 13"x9" baking pan; bake at 325 degrees for 30 minutes or until toothpick inserted in center removes clean. Cool; frost before serving. Makes 12 to 15 servings.

Icing:

8-oz. pkg. cream cheese,
   softened

2 c. powdered sugar
1 c. flaked coconut

Mix together until smooth and creamy.

Sometimes the heart sees what is invisible to the eye.
–H. Jackson Brown, Jr.

Texas Sheet Cake

Marylyn Morell
Cleveland, OH

No one can resist this rich, fudgy cake...it's decadent!

1 c. butter, softened
4 T. baking cocoa
1 c. water
2 c. all-purpose flour
2 c. sugar
1 t. baking soda

1 t. salt
1 t. baking powder
1 c. sour cream
2 eggs
1 t. vanilla extract

Combine butter, cocoa and water in a 5-quart saucepan; bring to a boil. Remove from heat; stir in flour, sugar, baking soda, salt and baking powder until well mixed. Add sour cream, eggs and vanilla; beat well. Pour into a greased and floured jelly roll pan; bake at 350 degrees for 20 minutes. Frost while warm. Makes 12 to 15 servings.

Frosting:

4 T. milk
6 T. butter, softened

3 T. baking cocoa
1-1/3 c. powdered sugar

Blend ingredients together in a mixing bowl until smooth.

Reminisce by listening to music by Connie Francis, Andy Williams, the Everly Brothers, Mickey & Sylvia, Fats Domino and Bobby Darin.

SALMON

PATTY'S

All the best from the Pacific Northwest.

Overnight Breakfast Rolls

Alyssa Derrington
Lexington, KY

Fix these yummy rolls the night before, then bake the next morning...what could be easier?

3 T. butter, melted
1 c. brown sugar, packed
1/2 c. chopped pecans

12 frozen dinner rolls
1/2 pt. whipping cream

Combine butter and brown sugar together; press into the bottom of a 13"x9" baking dish. Sprinkle with pecans; arrange frozen rolls on top. Pour whipping cream over rolls; cover tightly with aluminum foil and set aside overnight at room temperature. Bake at 350 degrees for 30 minutes; cool 10 to 15 minutes. Serve rolls by turning them over onto a plate so the sauce is on top; drizzle any remaining sauce over rolls, as desired. Makes 12 servings.

Travel tip: have some melody fun...one player hums the tune from a TV show or commercial and the other players have to guess the name of the product or TV show. The first player to guess correctly thinks of the next tune!

SALMON
PATTY'S

Sweet Jam Biscuits

Cathy Simmonds
Cincinnati, OH

Use your family's favorite flavors of jam for these tasty biscuits.

12-oz. can flaky refrigerated
   biscuits
1/4 c. butter, melted

1 c. sugar
1 T. cinnamon
4 T. raspberry jam

Separate biscuits; dip into butter. Sprinkle with sugar and cinnamon; place in a 9" round baking pan. Make a thumbprint in the center of each biscuit; fill with one teaspoon of jam. Bake at 375 degrees for 16 to 18 minutes; let cool several minutes before serving. Makes 10 servings.

The road to a friend's house is never long.
-Danish proverb

Patty's Hashbrown Casserole

Angela Rorrer
Hanover, PA

This speedy breakfast is a crowd pleaser!

30-oz. bag frozen hash browns, partially thawed
10-3/4 oz. can cream of mushroom soup

2-1/2 c. shredded Cheddar cheese
2 T. butter, melted

Mix ingredients together; spread into a 13"x9" baking dish. Bake at 350 degrees for 30 to 40 minutes. Makes 12 to 15 servings.

Motoramas were popular in years past...go to a car show and set your sights on a dream car.

SALMON PATTY'S

Apples & Potatoes

Kathy Grashoff
Fort Wayne, IN

*Serve this dish with scrambled eggs for breakfast
or pork chops for dinner.*

4 potatoes, peeled and cubed
2 apples, peeled, cored and
   sliced
1 T. sugar

4 slices bacon, chopped
1 onion, sliced
1 T. butter, softened and sliced
1/8 t. nutmeg

In a 5-quart saucepan, bring one inch of water to a boil; add potatoes, apples and sugar. Bring to a boil again; reduce heat. Simmer, covered, until potatoes are tender, about 15 minutes; drain and set aside. In a skillet, fry bacon until crisp; drain, reserving drippings in skillet. Add onions to reserved drippings; sauté until tender. Place potato mixture into a serving dish; dot with butter. Sprinkle with nutmeg; top with bacon and onion. Serve warm. Makes 4 to 6 servings.

Listen for the tinkling bells of the ice cream truck heading up
your street on the next hot afternoon...run
out and get a cool treat!

Artichoke-Spinach Dip

Rebecca Boone
Olathe, KS

This dip is so easy to prepare...you'll get many requests for the recipe!

14-oz. can artichoke hearts, drained and chopped
1-1/2 c. mayonnaise
1-1/2 c. fresh Parmesan cheese, grated

4-oz. can diced green chilies, drained
1 clove garlic, minced
10-oz. pkg. frozen chopped spinach, thawed

Combine first 5 ingredients; mix well. Squeeze excess moisture from spinach using a paper towel; add to mayonnaise mixture. Spread into a greased 9" pie plate; bake at 350 degrees for 20 to 25 minutes. Serves 6.

A friendship can weather most things and thrive in thin soil but it needs a little mulch of letters and phone calls and small, silly presents every so often...just to save it from drying out completely.

–Pam Brown

SALMON PATTY'S

Pine Cone Cheese Ball

Belinda Tanberg
Sacramento, CA

*For an even prettier presentation,
add a sprig or two of greenery to your serving plate.*

8-oz. pkg. cream cheese,
  softened
1/4 c. mayonnaise
2 green onions, chopped

4 slices bacon, crisply cooked
  and crumbled
3/4 t. dill weed
1 c. whole almonds

Combine first 5 ingredients; form into an almond shape. Layer almonds over the cheese ball to resemble a pine cone. Cover; chill before serving. Makes 1-1/2 cups.

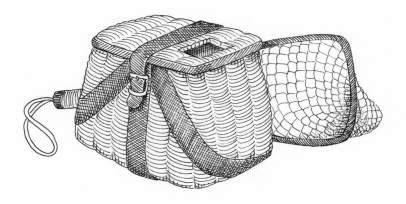

Consider exploring the San Juan Islands in the Pacific Northwest where you can island-hop all day. Visit towns with quaint shops and restaurants or fish and hike in unspoiled beauty.

Tuna Paté

Kim Johnston-Orazio
Derry, PA

Serve with a variety of shapes and flavors of crackers.

5 slices bacon, crisply cooked,
   crumbled and divided
2 8-oz. pkgs. cream cheese,
   softened
2 7-oz. cans water-packed tuna,
   drained and flaked

2 T. white wine
2 T. lemon juice
1 T. soy sauce
1 t. dill weed
2 T. dried parsley
1 green olive, sliced

Blend all ingredients together except one slice cooked and crumbled
bacon and olive. Place mixture onto a serving platter; mold into a fish
shape. Use reserved bacon for scales and an olive slice for an eye.
Makes 3 cups.

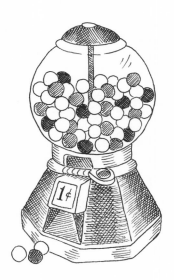

**Next time you're at the flea market, look for lunch boxes and
matching thermoses...just the right size for holding
odds & ends in the kitchen or craft room.**

SALMON
PATTY'S

Cheesy Crab Dip

Sheila Sawyer
York, PA

This dip is delicious served with crackers or crusty bread.

1 lb. crabmeat
2 8-oz. pkgs. cream cheese,
   softened
1 c. sour cream
4 T. mayonnaise
1/2 t. lemon juice

1 t. spicy brown mustard
1-1/2 t. garlic salt
1 t. seafood seasoning
3 t. Worcestershire sauce
1 c. shredded Cheddar cheese

Combine ingredients together; pour into a 1-1/2 quart casserole dish. Bake at 325 degrees for 45 minutes; serve warm. Makes about 4 cups.

Use seashells gathered during your vacation to frame your favorite vacation photo. Just use tacky glue to affix them to a frame...your memories of the beach are preserved!

Artichoke Squares

Sharon Miller
Dallas, TX

A flaky crust and three kinds of cheese make this appetizer disappear fast!

2 8-oz. cans refrigerated crescent rolls
1/2 c. onion, finely chopped
4 T. margarine
1 T. all-purpose flour
1/2 c. half-and-half
1/2 c. sour cream
4 eggs, beaten
1 t. salt
1/2 t. pepper
1/2 t. dill weed
1/4 t. nutmeg
1 t. dried parsley
2 9-oz. cans artichoke hearts, chopped
1 c. shredded Cheddar cheese
1 c. shredded Swiss cheese
1/2 c. grated Parmesan cheese

Unroll dough; press into bottom of a lightly greased 13"x11" baking dish to form a crust, save any excess for another recipe. Bake at 350 degrees for 7 minutes. Flatten baked dough with a spoon; return to oven and bake 5 more minutes, then cool. Sauté onion in margarine until tender; stir in flour and half-and-half until thickened. In a separate mixing bowl, combine sour cream, eggs, salt, pepper, dill, nutmeg and parsley; add to onion mixture. Place 1/2 artichoke hearts over crust; sprinkle Cheddar cheese on top. Layer remaining artichoke hearts over cheese; top with Swiss cheese. Pour on onion mixture; sprinkle with Parmesan cheese. Bake at 325 degrees for 45 minutes; cool and cut into squares. Makes 2 dozen.

An ideal summer resort is where the fish bite and the mosquitoes don't!
– Unknown

SALMON
PATTY'S

Smoky Salmon

Crystal Lappie
Worthington, OH

Our favorite family gathering appetizer...once you taste it,
you can't stop!

7-3/4 oz. can salmon
8-oz. pkg. cream cheese,
    softened

2 T. onion, minced
1/8 t. liquid smoke flavoring
2 T. fresh parsley, chopped

Drain and flake salmon; reserve 2 teaspoons of liquid. Combine reserved liquid with salmon, cream cheese, onion and liquid smoke; blend thoroughly. Refrigerate several hours; form into a 6 to 8-inch log. Roll in parsley before serving. Makes 2 cups.

A slicker hike in the rain can be fun on a trip or right at home...everything looks and sounds different after a sprinkle. Slosh along for a relaxing change of pace!

Rosie's Salmon Croquettes

Sandra Dodson
Indianapolis, IN

We love this recipe so much...it was the only way my mother could get my brothers and me to eat salmon!

6-oz. can pink salmon, undrained
2 eggs, beaten
1 t. salt

2 c. corn flake cereal, crushed and divided
1 t. baking powder
1/2 c. corn oil

Combine salmon with liquid, eggs, salt and 1/2 cup corn flakes; blend in baking powder. Shape into croquettes; roll into remaining corn flakes. Heat oil to 375 degrees in a 10-inch skillet; deep-fry croquettes. Drain on paper towel. Serves 4.

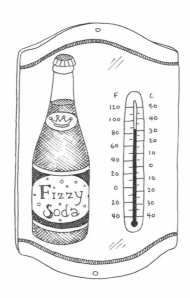

Enjoy the classic comics of Dick Tracy, Betty Boop, Blondie, Annie or Popeye again or for the very first time.

SALMON
PATTY'S

Mandarin Salad

Liz Hall
Worthington, IN

This fruity salad is a refreshing way to start a meal.

1 kiwi, sliced
1/2 head iceberg lettuce, torn
1/4 bunch Romaine lettuce, torn
1 c. celery, chopped
2 T. green onions, chopped
1/4 c. oil
2 T. vinegar

3 T. plus 1 t. sugar, divided
1/2 t. salt
1/8 t. pepper
1 T. fresh parsley, chopped
1/4 c. slivered almonds
11-oz. can mandarin oranges,
    drained

Mix together kiwi, lettuces, celery and green onion; store in large bag in refrigerator. Combine oil, vinegar, 2 tablespoons sugar, salt, pepper and parsley in an airtight jar; refrigerate. Sauté almonds and remaining sugar in a skillet over medium heat until well coated; cool and break apart. To serve, place lettuce in serving bowl and top with almonds and oranges. Shake dressing well; pour over the top. Makes 6 servings.

Dress up a mouth-watering coconut cake or
butterscotch meringue pie by placing it on an
old-fashioned pedestal plate.

Summer Risotto

Kathy Unruh
Fresno, CA

Serve this fresh side dish with grilled chicken or pork chops.

3 cloves garlic
2 shallots, chopped
3 T. olive oil, divided
2 c. arborio rice
1 qt. vegetable broth, divided
1 lb. asparagus, chopped
3 plum tomatoes, diced

2 T. fresh basil, chopped
1-1/2 c. canned corn
3/4 c. fresh Parmesan cheese,
   grated and divided
salt and pepper to taste
Garnish: zest of one lemon

Sauté garlic and shallots in one tablespoon olive oil until tender; add rice and sauté 2 minutes. Add enough broth to cover rice; cook, stirring constantly until broth is absorbed. Add remaining broth; heat until rice is al dente, 10 to 12 minutes. Add asparagus, tomatoes, basil and corn; stir in 1/2 cup Parmesan cheese and mix well. Season with salt and pepper to taste. Serve warm in a large bowl; toss with remaining olive oil, Parmesan cheese and lemon zest. Makes 4 servings.

Now and then it's good to pause in our pursuit
of happiness and just be happy.
– Guillaume Apollinaire

SALMON
PATTY'S

Scalloped Oysters

Mary Gadsby
El Cajon, CA

*Tender oysters in a creamy sauce will be a hit
at your next gathering.*

2 c. half-and-half
1/2 c. butter
1 t. salt
1/8 t. pepper

2 eggs, beaten
3 c. cracker crumbs
3 doz. oysters, undrained

Scald half-and-half with butter in a small saucepan; season with salt and pepper. Cool slightly; stir in eggs. Layer cracker crumbs, oysters and cream mixture into a buttered 1-1/2 quart casserole dish; bake at 350 degrees for one hour. Makes 6 to 8 servings.

**Display treasures of family trips...add souvenirs or seashells
and you'll always remember your vacation adventures.**

Northwest Noodle Salad

Kristen Gonzalez
Lebanon, PA

A refreshing alternative to traditional salad.

4 3-oz. pkgs. chicken flavored
   ramen noodles, crumbled
16-oz. bag broccoli coleslaw
1 c. oil

1/2 c. red wine vinegar
1/2 c. sugar
1/2 c. sunflower seeds
1/2 c. slivered almonds

Place noodles in bottom of shallow container; spread broccoli slaw on top and set aside. In a separate bowl, mix oil, vinegar, sugar and noodle flavor packets together; pour over noodles and slaw but do not mix. Cover and refrigerate for at least 18 hours; toss mixture with sunflower seeds and almonds before serving. Makes 10 servings.

Add a retro touch to any get-together with
vintage cocktail shakers and sets of glasses in wire
holders...look for them at flea markets and tag sales.

Baked Turkey Penne

Jaylene Wisor
Portland, TX

*Increase or decrease the amount of cayenne to adjust
the spiciness to your family's taste.*

3 cloves garlic, chopped
1 lb. ground turkey, browned
1/3 t. cayenne pepper
1 onion, chopped
28-oz. can peeled tomatoes,
   diced
1/3 c. pesto sauce

16-oz. pkg. penne pasta, cooked
   and drained
10 oz. spinach, torn
1/2 lb. mozzarella cheese, cubed
1 c. grated Parmesan cheese,
   divided

Sauté garlic, turkey, cayenne pepper and onion in a large saucepan until vegetables are tender. Add tomatoes; simmer until sauce thickens, stirring occasionally. Remove from heat; stir in pesto. In a large mixing bowl, combine pasta, spinach, mozzarella and 1/3 cup Parmesan cheese; pour in tomato mixture. Spoon into a lightly greased 13"x9" baking pan; sprinkle with remaining cheese. Bake at 375 degrees for 30 minutes. Makes 12 servings.

Remember the old-fashioned jukebox at the local diner?
Tune your radio to the oldies station and do the twist,
shag and jitterbug...just for fun!

Spinach–Bacon Salad

Stephanie Buettner
Bellevue, NE

A very refreshing salad...whenever I take it to barbecues or parties, I always get so many compliments!

1 bunch spinach leaves, torn
8-oz. pkg. sliced mushrooms
1/2 red pepper, chopped
1 carrot, sliced

1/2 lb. bacon, crisply cooked and
  crumbled
2 green onions, chopped

Toss first 4 ingredients together; top with bacon and green onions. Serve with dressing. Makes 6 servings.

Dressing:

1/3 c. catsup
1/2 c. white vinegar
2/3 c. sugar
1 clove garlic, minced
salt and pepper to taste

1/2 c. olive oil
1/2 lb. bacon, crisply cooked and
  crumbled
1 green onion, chopped

Blend first 6 ingredients together until smooth; add bacon and green onion. Shake well.

Travel is ninety percent anticipation and
ten percent recollection.
– Edward Streeter

SALMON PATTY'S

Seafood Fettuccini

Lorena Freis
Waterloo, IA

Scallops or crab may be substituted for added variety.

3/4 lb. shrimp, cooked, peeled and deveined
4-oz. can mushroom stems and pieces, drained
1/2 t. garlic powder
1/8 t. salt
1/8 t. pepper
1/4 c. butter

8-oz. pkg. fettuccine, cooked and drained
1/2 c. grated Parmesan cheese
1/2 c. milk
1/2 c. sour cream
Garnish: 1/2 T. fresh parsley, chopped

Sauté shrimp, mushrooms, garlic powder, salt and pepper in butter for 3 to 5 minutes; stir in fettuccine, Parmesan cheese, milk and sour cream. Heat over medium until warmed; do not boil. Garnish with parsley. Makes 4 servings.

Make a wish list of things you want to do while traveling so getting there is truly half the fun.

Chicken-Cheddar Wraps

Jamie Davis
Fremont, CA

This is a great way to use leftover
chicken...it'll become a family favorite.

1 c. sour cream
1 c. salsa
2 T. mayonnaise
4 c. cooked chicken, cubed
2 c. shredded Cheddar cheese

1 c. sliced mushrooms
2 c. lettuce, shredded
1 c. guacamole
12 flour tortillas
Garnish: tomato wedges

Combine sour cream, salsa and mayonnaise; add chicken, cheese and mushrooms. Divide lettuce between tortillas; top with 1/4 cup chicken mixture on each tortilla. Spread with guacamole; roll up tortilla. Place tortillas on serving dish; garnish with any remaining guacamole and tomato wedges. Makes 12 servings.

Share fond childhood memories with your own
children...tell them about Captain Kangaroo,
Mr. Green Jeans and Dancing Bear.

SALMON
PATTY's

Sunny Day Casserole

Joy Schulz
Clintonville, WI

This creamy, cheesy casserole is perfect with
hearty meat loaf and mashed potatoes.

11-oz. can shoe peg corn,
   drained
14-1/2 oz. can French-style
   green beans, drained
10-3/4 oz. can cream of celery
   soup

3/4 c. sour cream
1 c. shredded Cheddar cheese
1/4 c. onion, diced
1 sleeve buttery round crackers,
   crushed
6 T. butter, melted

Combine first 6 ingredients; pour into a 2-quart baking dish and set
aside. Mix crushed crackers and butter in a mixing bowl; spread over
casserole. Bake at 350 degrees for 30 to 45 minutes. Makes
6 to 8 servings.

Create your own summertime water playground with a
sprinkler, squirt guns and water balloons!

Picnic Pasta Salad

Elizabeth VanEtten
Warwick, NY

This pasta salad is a quick dinner for
busy families...you prepare it the day before!

16-oz. bag tri-colored pasta,
   cooked and drained
1 c. onion, diced
1 c. celery, chopped
1 c. sliced black olives
1/2 c. green olives, sliced
1 red pepper, thinly sliced
1 green pepper, thinly sliced

1/2 c. fresh parsley, chopped
1/2 c. fresh dill, chopped
1 T. minced garlic
1 T. fresh oregano, chopped
1 c. lemon juice
1-1/2 c. olive oil
salt and pepper to taste

Toss pasta with onion, celery, olives and peppers; set aside. Mix remaining ingredients together; pour over pasta. Cover and refrigerate at least a day before serving. Serves 6 to 8.

Travel tip: Partially freeze bottles of fruit juice and water, then pack them in your picnic cooler to help keep your snacks cold...when lunch is served, the juice will be ready to drink!

SALMON
PATTY'S

Dilly Salmon Pasta Sauce

Brenda Doak
Gooseberry Patch

Serve over angel hair pasta or thin spaghetti.

3 T. butter
3 shallots, finely chopped
1 lb. smoked salmon, thinly
    sliced

3 c. whipping cream
1/2 cucumber, finely chopped
4 T. fresh dill, chopped
1 t. white pepper

Melt butter in a large saucepan; sauté shallots until tender, 2 to
3 minutes. Add salmon; sauté 2 to 3 minutes more. Remove salmon
and shallots to a platter; add cream to same saucepan. Bring to a boil
over moderate-high heat; gently boil 15 to 20 minutes. Return salmon
and shallots to saucepan; gently boil 2 minutes. Stir in cucumber, dill
and pepper. Serve warm over pasta. Serves 4 to 6.

It is good to have an end to journey toward,
but it is the journey that matters in the end.
–Ursula K. LeGuin

Sweet & Sour Carrots

Sandra Whiting
Richland, WA

Equally delicious served hot or cold.

2 lbs. carrots, sliced
water
1/4 c. oil
1/4 c. sugar

1/4 c. vinegar
10-3/4 oz. can tomato soup
1 onion, diced
1 green pepper, chopped

Boil carrots in water until tender; drain and set aside. Mix remaining ingredients together in a small saucepan; simmer 10 minutes. Pour over carrots; stir gently. Makes 4 to 6 servings.

Remember listening to waitresses in their starched, pink uniforms placing orders with the cooks in their own lunch-counter lingo?

SALMON
PATTY'S

Egg Rolls

Patricia Taylor
Wellsville, PA

Try preparing these egg rolls with chicken, beef and shrimp too.

3 carrots, diced
2 onions, diced
2 T. oil
1 lb. pork, browned and chopped
3 T. soy sauce
3 T. sugar

14-oz. can bean sprouts, drained
  and rinsed
8-oz. pkg. thin egg noodles,
  cooked and drained
16-oz. pkg. egg roll wrappers
oil for deep-frying

Sauté carrots and onions in oil until tender; add meat, soy sauce and sugar. Simmer 5 minutes; add bean sprouts and remove from heat. Chop cooked noodles; add to vegetable mixture. Spoon filling into egg roll wrappers; fold burrito-style. Deep-fry until golden; turning once. Makes about 12.

Greet your mail carrier with a frosty fifty-five
(glass of root beer) on a hot, humid summer day.

Strawberry-Yogurt Shake

Marian Buckley
Fontana, CA

A fresh and fruity way to start the day.

1 c. strawberry yogurt
1 c. milk

3 ice cubes
1 c. frozen strawberries

Combine all ingredients in a blender; blend until smooth. Makes 4 servings.

Red Chili Chips

Vickie

These spicy, made-from-scratch potato chips are so tasty when dunked in ranch dip!

3 Idaho potatoes, thinly sliced
oil for deep-frying
1/2 t. chili powder

1/2 t. cayenne pepper
1 t. onion salt
1/4 t. salt

Soak potato slices in ice water for 1/2 hour; drain and pat dry with paper towels. Deep-fry potato slices in 350 degree oil until golden; remove with slotted spoon, drain and place in serving bowl. Combine remaining ingredients; shake over chips. Toss to coat evenly; serve warm. Makes 8 servings.

If all the world were apple pie,

And all the seas were ink,

And all the trees were bread & cheese,

What would we have to drink?

– Mother Goose

SALMON
PATTY'S

Seattle Sandwich

Michelle Campen
Peoria, IL

You don't have to live near the Space Needle to enjoy this sandwich!

8-oz. pkg. cream cheese,
  softened
1/3 c. chopped walnuts
1 T. honey
6 slices multi-grain bread,
  toasted

6 leaves lettuce
6 slices smoked turkey breast,
  divided
1/2 c. whole-berry cranberry
  sauce

Combine cream cheese, walnuts and honey; spread on half the slices of toast. Top with lettuce, turkey breast, 2 tablespoons cranberry sauce and remaining slices of bread. Makes 3 sandwiches.

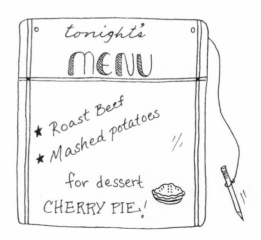

Travel tip: provide children with sweetened cereal rings and string licorice...they can string the cereal onto the licorice to make bracelets and necklaces. When they get hungry, they can snack on their creations!

Almond-Cherry Pie

Wendy Lee Paffenroth
Pine Island, NY

Sprinkle with slivered almonds before baking for added crunch.

1-1/2 c. vanilla wafer cookies, crushed
4 T. butter, melted
14-oz. can sweetened condensed milk

1 t. lemon zest
1 t. almond extract
1 c. sour cream
21-oz. can cherry pie filling

Combine cookie crumbs and butter together; pat into a greased 9" pie plate. In a mixing bowl, mix milk, zest, extract and sour cream together; beat well. Pour into pie crust; drop pie filling by tablespoonfuls onto sour cream mixture. Bake at 400 degrees for 18 to 20 minutes; cool and refrigerate. Makes 8 servings.

Any activity becomes creative when the doer cares about doing it right, or doing it better.
–John Updike

SALMON
PATTY'S

Rhubarb Torte

Sandy Lynch
Iroquois, SD

This tasty torte has a perfect balance of tart and sweet.

1-1/4 c. all-purpose flour,
    divided
1-1/2 c. plus 2 T. sugar, divided
1/2 c. margarine, softened
2 eggs, beaten

2-1/2 c. rhubarb, finely chopped
1/2 t. salt
3/4 t. vanilla extract
1/2 c. chopped nuts

Combine one cup flour, 2 tablespoons sugar and margarine together; press into a 9"x9" pan. Bake at 350 degrees for 20 minutes; cool. In a mixing bowl, blend remaining ingredients; pour over crust. Bake at 350 degrees for 30 minutes. Makes 16 servings.

To avoid ice cream drips in warm weather, tuck a
marshmallow inside the bottom of a sugar cone...it
will serve as a drip-stopper!

Oregon Hazelnuts

Janet Dodge
Blairstown, NJ

I have a friend who is a beekeeper...she supplies
the honey and I supply the nuts!

2/3 c. honey, warmed   2 c. powdered sugar
2 c. hazelnuts

Combine honey and hazelnuts; coat well. Spread onto a baking sheet; bake at 350 degrees for 12 to 15 minutes or until nuts begin to roast. Turn every 3 to 4 minutes; stirring often. Immediately pour nuts into a bowl with powdered sugar; toss to coat. Place on a clean baking sheet to cool; recoat with powdered sugar. Store in an airtight container. Makes 2 cups.

Relive the best of old-fashioned American summer
fun...run through the water sprinkler, sip a refreshing glass of
lemonade on the front porch and enjoy a game of horseshoes!

SALMON
PATTY'S

Island Tropic Muffins

Catherine Marie Taafe
Canfield, OH

Pair these fruity muffins with a steamy cup of herbal tea.

1 c. self-rising flour
1/4 c. sugar
1 egg, beaten
1/2 c. milk
1/4 c. oil

1/2 t. vanilla extract
1 c. maraschino cherries
1 c. flaked coconut
Garnish: cherries

Combine flour and sugar together; make a well in the center. Add remaining ingredients together except for coconut in a separate mixing bowl; pour into well, stirring until just moistened. Spoon into lined muffin cups; bake at 400 degrees for 13 to 15 minutes. Sprinkle with coconut last 5 minutes of baking time; top each with a cherry. Makes 12 muffins.

Vintage diner signs are a whimsical way to
decorate your kitchen walls...add a red checked
tablecloth to complete the setting!

Apple Pie Cake

Lisa Hays
Crocker, MO

*Also scrumptious served with a big scoop of
vanilla ice cream.*

1/2 c. butter
1 egg
1 c. sugar
1 t. cinnamon
1 c. all-purpose flour
1 t. salt

1 t. baking soda
2-1/2 c. apples, peeled and
    chopped
2 T. boiling water
1/4 c. chopped walnuts
Garnish: whipped topping

Cream butter, egg and sugar together; add cinnamon, flour, salt and
baking soda, mixing well. Toss apples, water and walnuts together in
a separate bowl; stir into flour mixture. Pour into a greased 9" pie
plate; bake at 350 degrees for 40 minutes. Serve with whipped
topping. Makes 8 servings.

Have a slice of the
good life! Ask for a
dollop of whipped
cream or a scoop
of French vanilla
ice cream with
your next slice of
apple pie.

SALMON PATTY'S

Mountain Range Sundae

Anna McMaster
Portland, OR

Kids absolutely adore this easy and delicious dessert.

20-oz. pkg. chocolate sandwich
  cookies, crushed
2 T. margarine, melted
1/2 gal. vanilla ice cream,
  softened

16-oz. can chocolate syrup
8-oz. carton whipped topping
Garnish: maraschino cherries,
  chopped nuts

Mix cookie crumbs and margarine together; pat into the bottom of a 13"x9" freezer-safe dish. Spread ice cream over the crust; pour chocolate syrup over ice cream layer and freeze. Top with whipped topping, cherries and nuts, if desired, before serving. Makes 12 to 15 servings.

Laughter is the shortest distance between two people.

–Victor Borge

Index

Index

Index

We've cooked up a
whole collection of
Gooseberry Patch®
books!

Have a taste for more? Call us toll-free at

1-800-854-6673

We'll send you our latest catalog filled
with snowmen, Santas, ornaments,
candles, cookie cutters, gourmet goodies,
calendars, giftwrap, pottery, collectibles
and MORE...including our best-selling
cookbooks!

Phone us:
1·800·854·6673

Fax us:
1·740·363·7225

Visit our website:
gooseberrypatch.com

Send us your favorite recipe!

*and the memory that makes it special for you!** If we select
your recipe for a brand new **Gooseberry Patch** cookbook,
your name will appear right along with it...and you'll
receive a FREE copy of the book! Mail to:
Vickie & Jo Ann
Gooseberry Patch, Dept. Book
600 London Road
Delaware, Ohio 43015
*Please include the number of servings and all other
necessary information!

TODAY'S SPECIALS 📖 BOTTOMLESS CUPS OF COFFEE ☕ BREAKFAST SERVED ALL DAY 🍳 FRIES ON THE SIDE 🍟 NEED A REFILL? 🥞 HOTCAKES 🍳 HASHBROWNS 🍔 CHEESEBURGERS & CONEY DOGS 🍩 STEAK & EGGS 🍳 MILKSHAKES & MALTS 🥤 MEATLOAF & MASHED POTATOES 🥯 BISCUITS & GRAVY 🥞